IF
OBAMA
HAD A
SON

THE TRUTH YOU'VE
NEVER THOUGHT ABOUT

BRANDON B. PORTER II

BBP3 Publishing
P. O. Box 70271
Memphis TN 38107
901 527-0182
www.bbp3publishing.com
bbp3publishing@gmail.com
www.brandonbporter.org

IF OBAMA HAD A SON

The Truth You've Never Thought About

ISBN: 978-0-578-15232-5

Printed in the US by Instant Publisher.

Front cover photography by Platon. Graphics design by Nicholas Howard and Whitney Rawls. Portrait of Author by Justin A. Shaw of www.jalanshawphoto.com

ACKNOWLEDGMENTS

I would like to express heartfelt thanks to my mother and father, who throughout my lifetime have provided through love the necessary direction and discipline; to my brother Bryson for constantly inspiring and motivating me to be the best big brother ever; to my grandparents for always giving me that extra comfort; to my friends for pushing me to be better than my best and sticking with me for the long run; and to my church family for being supportive and loving.

I especially would like to thank everyone who helped make this dream of a book a reality: To Phyllis Dearing, for your literary genius and precision in editing. You have been a total Godsend in this entire venture. To Willie Dearing, III, for your insightful, thought-provoking contributions. To Pastor Matthew Brown for your political savvy and gift to humanity. To my big brothers, Ronelle Jones and Andrew Singleton, for being there from start to finish and lending your creative perspectives. To Avril Fuller, Karen Reid, and Christopher Suell, Esq., and our entire staff for bringing teamwork to make the dream work.

Finally, but most importantly, I would like to thank God, my ultimate source, who gives me life and the strength to fulfill my destiny.

Table of Contents

Preface

Is it a boy or a girl? In the not-so-distant past— until the latter half of the twentieth century at least, before ultrasound technology took center stage—this question prevailed in delivery rooms as the most frequently asked question. The answer would bring the highest degree of anticipation for expecting parents all over the world. So much lay in the answer to this question. Imagine what must

> **In a boy lay the hope of the father's posterity.**

have transpired in the minds of hopeful parents as they awaited the cry of the infant that had just made an arrival into the world. In that doctor's hand could be the rise or fall of kingdoms, prolific scientific discoveries, medical breakthroughs, advancements in technology, theological expansions, and the proliferation of such. In the few seconds that the parents awaited the infant's cry—the first sound that would herald the birth of purpose—they understood that this miracle could one day effect the fate of many. In a girl was the promise of being able to bear seed and continue the process of replenishing the earth. In a boy lay the hope of the father's posterity.

The value of sons to the world has been noted since the beginning of civilization. Ancient kings preferred sons for obvious reasons. Royalty stayed within the family, and having sons was the only way that a king could procure his legacy. Ancient societies also welcomed the sons of kings. Even before the discovery of DNA, citizens overwhelmingly perceived the concept of nobility as a genetic trait, simply believing that "blue blood" was passed down from fathers to their sons. And, since sovereignty was equated with divinity, those ancient societies not just embraced, but also heavily depended upon royal procreation.

Only in the event of a threat would dissent arise concerning a king's legacy. Some societies have been known to overthrow kings and their families when they thought the king's rule to be too dictatorial. Others sought to silence whole royal families when the monarchy became too powerful. A more subtle method of disrupting a dynasty would be to cause a cessation of the family line. Daughters posed little threat, but a male child, even in his infancy, could become a target. Even religious history testifies to this supposition. History records several incidents where kings would kill the sons of other kings to stop future threats. Even King Herod did not want God to have a Son! A defense mechanism not limited to ancient kingdoms or the Bible, the silencing of sons still exists in theory. It wasn't long ago that this phenomenon occurred right here in the United States of America with the rise and subsequent fall of powerful political leaders.

Biblically speaking, I see something in these words: "Nation shall rise against nation and kingdom against kingdom" (Matthew 24.7). But allow me to transpose this verbiage with more contemporary application: culture against culture, race against race, political parties against political parties, etc. In all of these destructive wars that were foreshadowed here, the ammunition remains the same—the silencing of sons. This annihilation does not necessarily involve actual killing (though not completely obsolete) but is often carried out by censoring, suppressing, and subjugating through methods that involve fear and intimidation. Notice the mysterious disappearance of our nation's sons. One

> **One generation after another has witnessed the near extinction of the offspring of some of our greatest political, civic, and social leaders.**

generation after another has witnessed the near extinction of the offspring of some of our greatest political, civic, and social leaders.

Am I suggesting conspiracy? Not necessarily. However, I simply want to begin this discourse by suggesting that, instinctively, we recognize that greatness is hereditary. Like brown eyes or intelligence, the power that one has to impact his or her environment transfers from one generation to the next—from parents to their children. If the father is a charismatic motivator, his son will more than likely possess a very similar personality trait. Though many people welcome the reproduction of talent, prowess, and authority; some people, like those ancient societies I mentioned earlier, may feel intimidated by people with the ability to exercise insurmountable influence on a nation. When people react in response to their fears, humanity suffers. For, fear leads to the onset of various societal issues, like racial divide, judicial imbalance, and political unrest.

In my attempt to reveal an unspoken truth, I want this book to enable better understanding, to encourage higher sensitivity, and ultimately to effect the emergence of a stronger, more productive generation.

Introduction

Most men crave sons because sons continue another twist of legacy. A son looks like his dad more and more each day. Though fathers are not offended by the birth of a girl, most are filled with desire and anticipation for that of a boy. A son, unlike a daughter, is more of a realistic extension of themselves...just like being cloned. The birth of a son is like one's life being extended beyond measure. I believe that there is no greater feeling to a father than to know that he has a son ready to take his place and continue his legacy. Having a son is the father's ultimate preparation for retirement and death. A son is the work of art that a man is blessed to leave behind or even his gift to the world.

> **Though fathers are not offended by the birth of a girl, most are filled with desire and anticipation for that of a boy.**

If President Obama had a son, how would that have affected his election? In the midst of all the fanfare celebrating his election and especially at the sight of the

First Family walking into the White House, I couldn't help but wonder what it would look like to have a young Barack Obama Junior in the procession.

As all Americans look on the First Family, some of us look and wonder how the United States would react to the son of the first African-American President. It may seem trivial to deal with the hypothetical "if Obama had a son" because he doesn't. But the President himself has dealt with this hypothetical saying, "If I had a son...." I, along with the President, can imagine what his son would look like. He would be the "mini-me" of his father: athletic, charismatic, eloquent, and strategic. Obama's son would keep his eye on the current news, and he'd be careful not to become it. We could imagine him straight and tall with swag, groomed for world-class leadership.

> **What would it mean to Americans to allow a black boy to become a man in the White House?**

While brooding over my imaginations of Obama Jr., I sense the real hostility toward young black males. While President Obama experienced plenty of hostility, he found favor with the American people in the midst of the nation's most desperate period of war and recession in the twenty-first century for many reasons, but two of those reasons are that he is not too young and he does not have a son. So I have peculiar questions bumping around in my head: What would it mean to Americans to allow a black boy to become a man in the White House? Would we even allow it? And what does it reveal about our nation that we went berserk at the President just mentioning, "If I had a son"?

I am the son of a prominent man, and I know the pain, the pressure, and the power of my position as his posterity. (I heard my dad say once that when you have a prominent father, you inherit some of his friends but all of his enemies.) The pain and the pressure come from a multitude of people and expectations in various realms: family, community, society, etc. But the power comes from my birthright as my father's oldest son. My social capital comes from my father's tutelage, networks, investments, and savings, which are compounded by the tutelage, networks, and so forth of his father. My father's name gives me access to people, places, and information that I have not earned access to. People seem to understand that privileging me with the access in the name of my father is as though they are privileging my father because I and my father are one; in other words, I am my father's extension—I am his son.

Yet, with all this privilege I have inherited, I still deal with an inheritance from my father that counters my privilege—I am black. My privilege hasn't completely protected me from prejudice. And while people in my family and in my community have high expectations, the larger society has low expectations for me. For, in our nation's history, systemic racism continuously cramps and cuts off the ability of black fathers to raise sons who will carry or create a legacy of strong political and moral influence. I have to discern whether the hurdles I encounter spring from personal responsibility or society's culpability so that I know how to leap over them to keep my birthright long enough to pass it on.

But I am here, and I am a man trained by my father, living his legacy. This is not so for the if-I-had-a-son of President Obama, who, at the thought of him, causes controversy and reveals the heart of a nation toward its sons.

PART ONE

THE SIGNIFICANCE

OF

SONSHIP

CHAPTER 1

The Riddle

My father and I were having a discussion some time ago as we would often do. This time, however, it was one of those "legacy" talks, where he would say things like, "Son, I won't always be here; and when the day comes that I have to leave this earth, you and your brother Bryson will have to continue for me." I often despised those talks, like most sons would, because at the time I practically viewed my father as an immortal hero. Upon hearing him say, "I won't always be here," I felt chills down my spine as I, for the first time in my life, thought about the burden of sonship. At that precise moment, I was forced to realize that not only do good things come to an end, but great people as well.

During those discussions with my dad, he would tell me things his father told him like, "Don't get bitter; get better," and "Your attitude determines your altitude." He would also recap how my grandfather, his late father, Bishop W. L. Porter, who too was a prominent religious leader, would never be forgotten as long as he (my father) was alive. During this particular discussion, my father suggested that my brother and I had the same responsibility. He shared how he wanted my brother and me to surpass his personal success by building on the legacy, which is simply what one leaves behind. Nearing the end of the discussion, my father shared a riddle with me that unveiled the privileges and challenges of sonship and legacy: "What is the one thing the most powerful man in the world wishes he had, but if he had it, he would never have been the most powerful man in the world?"

> **Barack Obama is indeed the most powerful man in the world simply because he is the President of the United States of America.**

Upon hearing my father's riddle, I was baffled and perplexed as most people are when they hear most riddles. And in the absence of a plausible answer, I followed the natural course with my much anticipated reply, "Ok, I give up. I don't know. What?" Of course, his answer to the riddle is now obvious—thus the title of this book. But behind that answer was the provocation of thought, which served as the inspiration for this entire discourse.

I must begin by noting that Barack Obama is indeed the most powerful man in the world simply because he is the President of the United States of America. The US President is considered the leader of the free world due to the economic and military position of the United States of America among the nations. His pedigree, inclination, intellect, occupation, or ethnicity does not matter. He could be an articulate scholar like Thomas Jefferson, a Hollywood actor like Ronald Reagan, a war hero like Ulysses S. Grant, a peanut farmer like Jimmy Carter, a bachelor like James Buchannan, an alcoholic like Andrew Johnson, or a gambler like Warren Harding. From our first President, George Washington, to our current Commander in Chief, Barack Obama, each of our 44 Presidents during his administration was considered the most powerful man in the world simply because he held the highest office in the world's most powerful country.

When Barack Obama ran for US President, he faced his share of opposition, as all presidential candidates do, but his run was unique for one very obvious reason. For the first time in American history, a black man was campaigning for the highest office in the land with a likelihood of winning, evident in the fact that

he was the first black candidate to win the democratic primary. Though it was clear that some vehemently opposed the idea of his being elected, others were perhaps on the fence, weighing the pros and the cons of giving a black man so much power. But along with his charisma, political savvy, wit, and intellect, there was one fact

If a would-be son could be perceived a threat to the future of America, why wouldn't his daughters?

about Barack Obama that may have tipped the scales in his favor: he had no sons.

I believe that a prevailing subconscious thought among voters who both opposed and favored our nation's 44th President was, "What if Obama had a son?" I follow this thought with several other questions of my own: Would Obama's son have been perceived as a potential threat? Could our nation even stomach the notion of a black male child growing up in the White House? What effect would a Barack Obama Jr. have on the future of the United States of America?

Though these questions are intriguing food for thought, the fact remains that President Barack Obama has no sons, but only daughters. In light of this fact, a more realistic supposition would suggest that Sasha and Malia could very well follow in their father's footsteps. If a would-be son could be perceived a threat to the future of America, why wouldn't his daughters? I have, what I believe to be, a logical response to this question; but first my disclaimer.

In no way am I asserting that a woman could not or would never become the leader of the free world. I do understand that there is a strong possibility that the 45th US President could very well be a woman. Moreover, in years to come, when Sasha and/or Malia will have met all qualifications for presidency, it is very possible that more than one woman will have had a stint in the Oval Office. But despite this rationale, it is highly unlikely for citizens to perceive Obama's girls as a superior threat in this day and age since we tend to base our judgments, and hence our fears, on precedents.

Let's examine the facts. Powerful women worldwide have been few, especially in the political realm. To date, the United States of America has never elected a woman as President. And along with the fact that all of the US Presidents have been men, at least twice in our nation's history, former Presidents witnessed the election of their sons and namesakes: John Quincy Adams and George W. Bush. Realizing that history has an uncanny way of repeating itself, coupled with the notion that human beings are unrelenting creatures of habit, a hypothetical Barack Obama Jr. would indeed be perceived as a threat by some as opposed to either daughter of our current President.

"Why a threat?" you may ask. I believe that the measure of power and influence that a person has can determine his or her fate because power is strength, and influence is the ability to lead. World History supports the belief that humanity allows an individual and/or that individual's family to possess and utilize only a certain degree of dominance. Even though Barack Obama was twice elected to the White House, the majority had no intention of allowing this Commander in Chief to pass down his influence to another generation of Obamas. Again, where voters might have found safety in the prospects of his daughters, I am convinced that they never would have felt so secure if Barack Obama had had a son.

> **This book is less about Barack Obama and more about the fear of legacy...**

24

Yes, I firmly believe that not having a son secured Obama's presidency, but this book is less about Barack Obama and more about the fear of legacy and the preservation of one of the world's most valuable commodities—our nation's sons. Included in the list of great men who have planted and watered, contributing to the success of this country, are those of African American descent. In these days, there is a lot of negative light on young black men—more negative it seems than positive; but please allow me to argue the value of these not often mentioned sons of America, without suggesting the reduction of value of those in other ethnicities.

The next time you are called upon by the Red Cross to donate a pint of blood, think about Dr. Charles Drew, the African American who in 1938 developed the blood banks that were instrumental in saving countless lives during World War II ("Charles Richard Drew"). The next time you crave a peanut butter and jelly sandwich, remember George Washington Carver, a former slave who, in 1880 not only reinvented this tasty lunch, but also discovered other products—including soap, dyes, and gasoline—that he made from using peanuts and other plants ("George Washington Carver"). The next time you are halted at a traffic light at a busy intersection—before you beat the steering wheel and let out your favorite expletive—reflect on Garrett Morgan, who on November 20, 1923, received a patent for his traffic signal invention. Not only did this African American revolutionize the traffic industry, but his discoveries led to what we now know as gas masks, the sewing machine, and the pressing comb for hard to manage hair ("Garrett Augustus Morgan Sr."). There are many other black Americans that we can thank for making our lives easier and/or more pleasurable with their clever inventions. Among them are Otis Boykin, whose invention in 1959 revolutionized TVs, radios, and pacemakers; Lonnie G. Johnson, who gave us the Super Soaker water gun in 1982; and George Crum, who, on August 24, 1853, was responsible for creating everyone's favorite comfort snack—potato chips ("Famous Black Inventors"). I believe that this if it were not for the suppression of African American men in this country, we would see more of these contributions to our society and the world.

When animals face extinction, we move heaven and earth to save them. I saw a report on the news concerning the fate of the bat. Yes, bats! Evidently, bats have been dying in record numbers from a disease that affects their ability to fly and feed. Though many are annoyed by them, scientists are searching feverishly for a cure that will resurrect the bat population (Dahler). The same type of commitment extends to whales, tigers, and other animals. I agree that saving animals from extinction is a great cause; however, I firmly believe that just as we work to preserve wildlife to allow those creatures to fulfill their several purposes within their ecosystems, we should invite healthy conversation to perpetuate understanding that would ultimately end the silencing of our sons in America.

President Obama has launched "My Brother's Keepers": a campaign to collaborate efforts from social, religious, and civic groups to discuss the healthy perpetuation of the black and Hispanic communities. I applaud the President's efforts and encourage other young people like myself to embrace his cause, which has the potential to last beyond his administration. More than ever, we need to remind ourselves that we are responsible for more than just ourselves to keep us from losing another generation.

> **More than ever, we need to remind ourselves that we are responsible for more than just ourselves to keep us from losing another generation.**

Again, that's what this book is about. It's a discussion that deals with the survival of sons and the embracing of daughters. It examines the imbalances of justice. It advocates the respect of all mankind and the love for humanity. It encourages family values and the strengthening of America's youth. It's about loving our neighbors by respecting their differences. This book anticipates the rise of coming generations by highlighting the importance of a family legacy that is characterized by a reputable family name.

CHAPTER 2

The Name You Know

In our culture, having a son is more about immortalizing the name than anything else. Throughout the ages names have always been important. Names reveal identity, and identity reveals intent. For example, the office of a porter, or in Old French *portier*, was a hereditary occupation for those who worked as gatekeepers in royal castles and monasteries; thus the surname "Porter" emerged to represent the families to which it was ascribed. Likewise, we have the Bakers, the Shoemakers, the Smiths, the Carpenters, the Hunters, the Farmers and the Fishers among many, many others. So a person's last name says much about his heritage. Custom teaches us to pass the father's name to their children and to their children's children. Girls eventually marry and take on their husbands' names while the boys keep the name alive in the family. In most cases, in the absence of sons, the family name eventually fades. Therefore, when a man wants to have a child with his mate, the first thing he wants to have is a boy because he knows that a boy has a possibility of carrying on his surname—thus the family legacy.

Although the familial occupation aspect is an antiquated concept, one's family name does speak to the success of the family. However, a person can very well be stigmatized just as quickly as he or she is praised. In our times, the name can also speak to the negativity or defamation of the family. But all too important is the fact that the name is what you make of it, not on the terms that you receive it. On that note, I am reminded of an old movie my father told me about, entitled *The Distinguished Gentleman*, which starred comedian Eddie Murphy. Since the movie plot fit so well in this chapter and the idea that I am suggesting, I thought that it would be befitting to share it with you.

Eddie Murphy's character was a hustler or scam artist who was always looking for his next scam. He did everything from network marketing to phone sex. Then, one day, he stumbled upon a scam that literally fell into his lap. For you see, his character's name was Thomas Jefferson Johnson. In the movie, Thomas Jefferson Johnson was watching television and saw a commercial where the candidate running for US Congress was a veteran politician by the name of Jeff Johnson. Jeff Johnson was a bit of a scam artist himself, just on a higher political level. The difference was that Eddie Murphy's character was African American; Jeff Johnson, the politician, portrayed by James Garner, was white American.

Jeff Johnson had served many years in Washington and had received much financial gain as a part of his scam artistry in government. In the midst of his campaign, this married aging politician had a heart attack and died while having extramarital relations with his secretary, leaving his seat vacant. At first, it was thought that his wife would make a run for his seat, but remember that Eddie Murphy's character first became familiar with Jeff Johnson through his candidacy. The commercial made a statement that stuck in Murphy's head like a stick in the mud: "Jeff Johnson, the name you know…." Upon hearing that, immediately a light came on: "If I drop Thomas and shorten Jefferson to Jeff, I am the name you know, "Jeff Johnson." And so he embarked upon his next scam, a run for United States congressman.

I am not saying that all US congressmen are scam artists, but in this movie this is how he was portrayed. So he ran, and he won. With new scam in hand, Eddie Murphy's character set off for our nation's Capitol. The funny thing about a name is that, as I previously stated, it reveals identity; and identity reveals intent. Although he went with a scam in hand as Jeff Johnson, Thomas Jefferson Johnson showed up later in the movie as a replica of our 3rd President, Thomas Jefferson, who was a great statesman and representative of the people. Yes, through the restructuring of his name, Thomas Jefferson Johnson transformed his character from

31

the dishonorable Jeff Johnson to the honorable Thomas Jefferson. He identified and sought to correct his scamming ways so that instead of working for himself, he was working for the people whom he represented. In the process, he truly distinguished himself as a gentleman and also found true love.

George Santayana said it best when he stated, "Those who cannot remember the past are condemned to repeat it." Part of the problem in today's society is that today's generation does not know its history; for deeply embedded in the history of African American culture are the names of great men who made many great advances for the African American people. However, the lack of knowledge, or ignorance of our history, has caused us to lose pace and has set us back in time. Knowing our history causes us to know the names that are connected to great accomplishments: Frederick Douglas, W.E.B. Dubois, A. Phillip Randolph, Charles H. Mason, Booker T. Washington, Ralph Bunche, Colin Powell, Andrew Young, John Lewis, John H. Johnson, Willie Gary, Arthur Ashe, Hank Aaron, Michael Jordan, Earvin "Magic" Johnson, etc. So we must remember those

However, the lack of knowledge, or ignorance of our history, has caused us to lose pace and has set us back in time.

names so that we can continue to move forward and achieve, accomplish, and advance—not just for ourselves but for future generations.

A fundamental principle concerning the importance of the name exits within our culture and becomes abundantly clear when we observe the lives of celebrated people within our political arena. Former U.S. President Bill Clinton had no sons, but he made such a lasting impact during his presidency that America began to crave the Clinton legacy. I suppose that Bill's wife Hillary has been so well received as a possible future presidential candidate partly because of her connection with him; it's the Clinton name that people adore. Notice how before her political career began she was known as Hillary Rodham Clinton, carrying her maiden name. Now, however, using the theory of *the name you know,* she is simply known as Hillary Clinton. The same is true for

Caroline Kennedy Schlossberg has become the political voice of the Kennedy family by default of her brother, her father's namesake, who was killed in a plane crash, thereby thwarting his political advancement.

the daughter of John F. Kennedy. Caroline Kennedy Schlossberg has become the political voice of the Kennedy family by default of her brother, her father's namesake, who was killed in a plane crash, thereby thwarting his political advancement. Upon the death of their uncle, Ted Kennedy, Caroline has had to take up the reigns of the family name. So while she uses her husband's last name, she still has to carry her father's name to keep the name of the Kennedy heritage alive.

> **The expectation of the father is that his son will not only continue his name but also his work.**

Mind you, my intention is not to defer from these women in any way, for they have made great accomplishments in their public careers, but they are not sons, nor do they have the ability to produce a name carrying seed. So once their fire has been extinguished, the name dies with them so that, while there is a story to be told, it becomes more legend than legacy. For, a legend comes to an end, but a legacy lives on.

In the case of the Kennedy family, there are sons (of brothers, etc.) who carry the name, yet by either choice or default of some sort, these men are not as in the forefront as JFK's daughter Caroline. Consequently, unless or until they produce a seed that will make great political strides for which this family name is known, the shoulder of responsibility lies upon her.

We must understand that whether the name comes from that of an occupation or nobility, the mantle of identity reveals the intent or purpose for one's life. As in most cases, the expectation is that the eldest son, if not all sons, will follow in the footsteps of the father— whether a policeman, politician, physician, or preacher. The expectation of the father is that his son will not only continue his name but also his work. I am my father's eldest son, and though he doesn't push me or prey on me to be a preacher, one of his greatest dreams or expectations is that I will follow in his footsteps.

CHAPTER 3

Next in Line

The relationship of a son to his father can compare to no other. For thousands of years, dynasties around the world have been founded upon the birth of a son. Fathers take absolute pride in the molding of their "justified remix," or "Jr." A son finds his own identity in the image of his father and finds responsibility in the longevity of his last name. Not a day passes by that I look in the mirror and do not see the face of my father. I often find myself speaking, writing, and conducting business like him more as time goes by. We become what we think about, and so many times sons of great expectations are burdened with the thought of not living up to the name of their fathers. This is the exact reason that sons find themselves acting more like their fathers each day. The thought of failure has bombarded their thought process to the point where they have to be precisely like their fathers, or better, to uphold and bestow honor to their families.

I am reminded of one of the hardest periods within my life so far. It was during my freshman year in college, beginning at the moment I stepped foot onto the Morehouse campus. I watched my parents drive away from my campus, looking back at their son who was now standing at the wheel of the world to make decisions of his own after eighteen long years of training and guidance for this very day. Before my mother, father, brother, and uncle pulled off, my father hopped out of the car, walked up to me, and said these words: "Son, you are on your own now; we can no longer be here to cover and protect you. It is time for you to start understanding the responsibilities of a man and accepting the responsibilities of your name. You are named after me; everything you do reflects an image of your family and me. Your little brother is watching everything you do and wants to be just like you. You

> **...So many times sons of great expectations are burdened with the thought of not living up to the name of their fathers.**

can't just be a follower when you were born to be a leader. Make us proud. I love you, Son. You're a Porter. Handle your business, and I'll see you soon." As I looked into his eyes with the fear of not seeing him again for months, I saw that there were tears forming around the bottom of his eyelids, and at that point I realized it was about more than just Brandon.

During those ten months, I was tested rigorously by the temptation of everything from drugs to suicide and anything else an 18-year-old college kid in the West End of Atlanta could be tested by. Sometimes, the pressure of wanting to be free had smothered me so deeply that I was ready to settle for being less than average, even if that meant stepping on my name. I got tired of people constantly calling me from all over for strength and advice to deal with the same temptations I was struggling with; when in all actuality, I was the one who was empty and looking for guidance. I was tired of being in an entirely different state where people still recognized my name and watched my every move to see if I would fail and give them one reason to trash my family name. I almost lost sight of who I was and what I stood for. At one point I came close to letting my father all the way down ... so much to the point where he was not just angry, but also disappointed and apprehensive about the direction of my future and his legacy in my hands. This feeling absolutely destroyed me on the inside because my father had been nothing short of great to me, and my only obligation was to go to school and make good grades. How could I let my father and mother down on something they had already given me the upper edge on?

The feeling of nearly failing him was so depressing that I felt as if all hope was lost for my future and that he would never trust me with the fate of our family legacy. But I had to understand that everyone makes mistakes; it's how you come back and learn from them that makes the difference.

One thing he commonly said began to play over in my head: "Son, never let your goal be what another man has to make you." At that point, I understood for myself that I had no other choice but to be a leader. For the first time in my life, I realized without somebody telling me ten times that I was not here on this earth for me but to help someone else and that I did not choose for it to be this way. God did. So if it is His will, it has to be done. Trying to escape it will only hinder me. Now, I do whatever it takes for me to stay on the right path to becoming the successful man I know I am destined to be. Staying focused gives me the leverage to learn from my mistakes, instead of becoming accustomed to making them. All I have to do is stay truthfully committed to being triumphant and know that I will walk into a great future.

Most times when the son applies himself, he succeeds. The father has already opened the door; all the son has to do is walk in and leave the key under the mat for the next generation. Imagine if this opportunity of succession had been existent for President Barack Obama in the White House. As a young promising, intelligent African American male, his son would be more popular, powerful, and threatening than most "established" politicians by the time he graduated high school. Just the thought is quite simply surreal—a young black boy running around the White House for eight whole years, entering as a naïve ten year old who gets saddened at the sight of his father boarding yet another flight on Air Force One to handle business for weeks across the globe. Yet, he exits as an eighteen-year-old man who now accompanies his father on boarding his plane because he now understands the awesomeness of his dad's responsibility to the world and that there is

> **The father has already opened the door; all the son has to do is walk in and leave the key under the mat for the next generation.**

now a strong possibility that his father's role as world leader could one day be his.

There is nothing more rewarding a son can give his father than a peace of mind in knowing that if any time he might leave this earth, everything will be just fine. Peace that the legacy paved by his blood, sweat, and tears would not be ruined. Peace that the family he has left behind would eat every night. Peace that generation after generation would continue to be prosperous by the works of his hands and the integrity of his last name. Last but not least, peace that his son would find the same contentment he had received.

On the morning of November 25, 1963, this nation received a most heartfelt visual glimpse of the special bond and relationship that a father has with his son. John F. Kennedy's son, J.F.K. Jr., or John-John, stood on the steps of St. Matthew's Cathedral on the day of his father's funeral, also his third birthday; raised his tiny hand no bigger than the size of a small baseball; lifted it to his head as his father had taught him only months before his assassination; and saluted him for one last time in front of the entire country ("Photographer Describes Capturing Iconic JFK Jr. Image"). This very brief moment in history was as though John-John was symbolically implying to the nation that his father might be slain physically; but … "his vision shall not die, his works shall not die, and hope for this country has not died; his legacy shall forever live through me, and his dream will forever be unfolded in the arms of this nation."

As a young, ambitious African American male in today's society, I have to make sure that I understand there is an obligation that I can no longer avoid. We are often underestimated and looked over in the world of politics and corporate America – not so much because of our skin color anymore, but because of the pitiful mindset we have embraced to make us psychologically poor.

> **The mind that Bill Gates possesses, yours has the same capacity.**

The mind that Bill Gates possesses, yours has the same capacity. The difference between the two of you is the amount of time he chooses to spend nurturing and exploring his. It is extremely simple to put together. In the words of Earl Nightingale, "We truthfully become what we think about." But Henry Ford said it best, "If you think you can do a thing, or you think you cannot do a thing, you are right."

So many times it is a limited mindset that imprisons young black males behind an enormous wall that is rarely broken down but by basketball and football. The human mind has an average of 50,000 thoughts that circumvent it each day. It only takes one of those 50,000 thoughts to be penetrated toward success, watered by studying, and put under the sunlight of wisdom from successful people in your equal field of interest; and that one thought could grow into the mindset that changes the life of more than 100,000 people that were in your same predicament.

> **There are no interstates or highways to success; you have to learn to take the streets.**

Being next in line is about more than just yourself; it is about giving someone else the assurance that he or she can make a difference in another's life, just as you made in his or hers. For what good is it for one to be successful if the knowledge is not relayed back to others on how to obtain the gift of prosperity?

When you are destined for greatness, you should not allow any mediocre mistakes to hinder you from achieving your goals. The challenge is not how many times you are knocked down; it's how many times you can stand back up and throw another punch. Take the time to sit and ponder on how many people are going after the same goals as you each day. Millions, right? Well, this is the difference that has to be established between them and you. There are no interstates or highways to success; you have to learn to take the streets. Yes, you will run into some red lights on the way, but they will always eventually turn green. Yes, you will encounter some stop signs, but don't turn around because you can eventually pass through. Yes, you will be honked at, but you cannot be discombobulated. Yes, you will drive past some accidents, but you cannot take your eyes off the road. Then before you know it, through all these interruptions, you will be pulling into the driveway of success while everyone else that tried to take the fast route is stuck in 5:00 traffic.

There is nothing new under the sun, but there is something precious, irreplaceable, and new in the birth of a son. As young men, we have to understand that we are next in line. Say what you will about Obama's presidency, but one thing is true: it established a precedent for the presence of future black sons in the White House—not for his hypothetical son, but for all of us, an entire nation of black sons. We are next in line for respect, next in line for greatness, and next in line for

45

legacy; but first we must prepare ourselves for transitioning.

CHAPTER 4

Lost Sons – Lost Legacy

Where are our nation's sons?

I believe that one of mankind's greatest calamities occurs when a misguided son fails to embrace the legacy of his father, specifically a father who has made an indelible imprint on humanity. As I expressed before, there is an expectation that greatness will pass down from one generation to the next. Society yearns to witness the rise of destiny's children. We don't want to forget the names of those who made significant deposits into our generation and generations before us. In our hearts, we want to embrace another Mandela, a King, a Roosevelt, a Lincoln, a Kennedy, an Eisenhower, a Cosby, a Sharpton, and a Gates among others. When certain people have impressed us, we can hardly fathom a world without them. However, understanding human mortality, we resign that even the lives of great men (and women) will eventually fade; so we look for them to reproduce greatness through their descendants. In America, however, there seems to have been, within the past few decades especially, an underlying antagonistic force that constantly interrupts the process of succession within powerful and/or influential families.

Notice how the sons of some of our most celebrated leaders have fallen off the scene.

Notice how the sons of some of our most celebrated leaders have fallen off the scene. For example, it would be an astonishing forty years after the death of Dr. Martin Luther King, Jr. before any one of his children would give him a grandchild, who just so happens to be a girl. It was as though King's family seemed afraid to reproduce – fearing retribution from enemies who could assassinate his body but could not assassinate his dream. Even more astounding is the fact that the renowned civil rights leader's daughter, Bernice King, has been far more vocal and visible, publicly and politically, than either of her brothers – a point that I will revisit later in this discourse. Jessie Jackson Jr., a once strong contender for the U.S. Senate and a probable future candidate for the presidency, was also silenced, imprisoned as a result of propaganda of embezzling campaign funds. The very influential Bill Cosby, a successful entertainer and one of the most revered fathers onscreen and off, lost his only son Ennis to a senseless homicide; another potential great silenced forever. I also found it interesting that Reverend Al Sharpton, who once put his bid in for US President and is currently a very outspoken voice for Civil Rights in the twenty-first century, has no sons to date to carry on his legacy. Perhaps, a more compelling, provocative account of the vanquishing of the male seed could be seen through the plight of the Kennedy family.

> **Perhaps, a more compelling, provocative account of the vanquishing of the male seed could be seen through the plight of the Kennedy family.**

When John F. Kennedy was killed, his family protectively covered his son JFK Jr., even so much that his sister Caroline was pushed more to the forefront than he was. But when he began to come forth in his adult years, he showed the same prospect of success and heart for people that his dad exhibited. But too quickly he was silenced by death so that the legacy of his father's seed could not continue through him. And though there yet remained other members of the Kennedy family, not one of them has operated at a level comparable to President Kennedy.

Senator Robert F. Kennedy, J.F.K.'s brother, was assassinated during his run for the presidency. Ted Kennedy, a younger brother, was also unsuccessful in his attempt to secure the highest office in the land. Although this Kennedy brother was quite visible in the political arena and adored by many until his death from cancer in 2009, scandals of drunkenness and misconduct seemed to dampen his influence throughout his political career. Robert F. Kennedy's son, Robert F. Kennedy, Jr., at age 14, greeted well-wishers as the train carrying his father's casket passed through on its way from New York to Washington, D.C. While doing so, he with pride wore his father's suit in display of allegiance to the legacy of his father. Yet, this young Kennedy has also faded into obscurity, doing things pertinent but not powerful, at least not politically.

When sons are absent, forgotten or silenced, legacies are lost.

Whether conspiracy or coincidence, it is evident that an undeniable, unfortunate pattern has existed among powerful and/or influential families within our nation. When sons are absent, forgotten or silenced, legacies are lost. This is unfortunate because, when the legacies of great men are lost, humanity mourns. Why? I am reminded of a story. Follow me on this one:

There lived a brave father who set out to save his city from villains that had plagued the people for centuries. This father had followed the footsteps of his father, who followed his father. He encountered a villain one day that was said to be the chief of them all, and although successful in his fight, his success came at the expense of his own life. The town buried the heroic young father but sorrowed with joy. They sorrowed with joy because they knew that he still had a son that could finish the work and destroy the less powerful villains that remained. The only problem was that the son was nowhere to be found; and, as a result, the problematic villains were still persistent and able to reproduce.

The African American community has buried its brave fathers who have taken down the chief villains such as segregation and slavery; but the less powerful villains, such as social and political injustices, inequality, racism, and the like, remain because the sons are lost and nowhere to be found. The blind stares of a million pairs of eyes look on as they wonder: Where are the lost sons? Where is the community's son that would stand up and continue the purging of a country from its twisted view that those of color are not as unique and humane as those of European, Mexican, Spanish, German, Jewish, Scottish, Swedish, or even Italian descent? Where is the community's son that would stand up and expose to this country the fact that we are all equal because we are all immigrants? Where is the community's son that would go into the White House not just for the rights of the American, but for the rights of the African American as well?

The answer to these questions cannot so easily be answered because the son that the community so eagerly awaits has now become a lost son among a newfound suppression. A perusal of the list of young fathers whom the community has buried will show that the list of sons is even greater. However, of all the sons that should have come forth, few have. The reasons the sons have not come forth are evident while unspoken and forbidden.

History's archives include a list of heroic fathers that fought valiantly and died, but whose sons were nowhere to be found.

History's archives include a list of heroic fathers that fought valiantly and died, but whose sons were nowhere to be found. One of the most notable champions of peace, equality, human rights, and inclusion is Abraham Lincoln, the 16th President of the United States of America ("Abraham Lincoln").

President Lincoln's compassion for the community in which he fought was so strong that it led to the abolishment of slavery and the Emancipation Proclamation in 1863. He used the army that he controlled as President to safeguard those slaves that had escaped from areas that were slow in honoring the new law; and he was also able to go into the territory of Congress and push, through all objections, the Thirteenth Amendment to the United States Constitution, which outlawed slavery forever. President Lincoln destroyed the villain known as slavery; but, like the young father in the aforementioned story, his victory came at the cost of his own life as he was assassinated on April 15, 1865. Like the son in the story who was nowhere to be found, Lincoln had four sons who would end up as lost sons as well.

Although Robert Todd Lincoln, the first son of President Lincoln, did not die prematurely, he never picked up where his father left off. He would live to be 82 but never put his hands on any issue, nor did he create an agenda that spoke to the issues that plagued the nation. President Lincoln's second son, Edward Baker Lincoln, died at the tender age of 3, just weeks before his 4th birthday. Little is known about baby Edward, so it's hard to tell whether he would have been the son to take up where his father left off. William Wallace Lincoln, like baby Edward, also died at a tender age; he was 11 years old. His cause of death was not certain, but it is believed that he died due to consuming water that was contaminated by the feces of soldiers who were situated by the Potomac River located by the White House at that time. President Lincoln's last son, Thomas Lincoln III, also died a premature death. Although Thomas hadn't had enough time to experience life, there are some characteristics to build upon that would be telltale signs of whether he would be "The Son," and if so, what kind of son he would be. It is said that Thomas was an impulsive, unrestrained child that refused to attend school and was homeschooled as a result. Rumor has it that Thomas was so cantankerous that his home-school teachers would quit out of frustration.

If Thomas were able to live to be "The Son," he would have been, in my opinion, unmoved and aggressive enough to take on the less powerful villains that remained after his father's death. However, that is not the case; and as a result, after the death of Lincoln, the community's brave father, there was no son to stand up and continue the fight. This phenomenon was echoed through the legacy of the great and honorable President John F. Kennedy (JFK), the 35th President of the United States of America. Like implied previously, he avidly fought for peace, equality, human rights, and inclusion.

President Kennedy exemplified his support of the African American through his endorsement of the Civil Rights Movement. He had been noted for saying that discrimination stained America as it led the West's moral stance against the Soviet Union during the Cold War. When Dr. Martin Luther King was arrested and put in jail in Georgia for driving with a license from another state, it was President Kennedy that made a call to Martin Luther King's wife that prompted the release of Dr. King from the Georgia jail. It was also Kennedy who came down on the federal government forcing them to employ more African American workers.

Prior to the force from President J.F.K., the FBI had only put 48 out of some 13,000 or so African American's to work. Although they were working, almost all 48 of those workers were drivers for white Americans. It is said and believed that Kennedy did more than any other President before him to get African Americans employed in the federal government sector.

Moreover, he was able to push for African Americans to be appointed as federal judges. Sadly, on November 22, 1963, in Dallas TX, President John F. Kennedy was also assassinated. He was killed by a gunman who was believed to be a part of a conspiracy that included "the death of President Kennedy."

Dissimilar to President Lincoln, President Kennedy had a son who lived to an age of maturity that would allow him to take the handles of the same plow his father held on to. However, after personal hindrances
that stemmed from a rocky marriage prevented John F. Kennedy, Jr. from running for the New York Senate seat or Governor of New York, he met his demise in a plane crash over the Atlantic Ocean on July 17, 1999. The death of young Kennedy Jr. would leave the community with yet another lost son. So much promise seen in a young man destined to be the son the community could look to as one to destroy the villains is stripped away through an unforeseen and untimely death. It was this same son whose image was captured in

> **The death of young Kennedy Jr. would leave the community with yet another lost son.**

a photo while saluting the body of his father, another son, as he was taken to his final resting place. As mentioned in chapter three, this image would send a message to the community that there was yet another son that remained that would stand up and bring justice to the community and triumph over the less powerful villains that still remained. Yet, suddenly this son was stripped from the community and left in what seemed to be another season of the lost son.

Among that list of young fathers who experienced the lost son syndrome is the great Malcolm X. Malcolm X's approach to fighting the less powerful villains was shunned by many more so because of the aggression in his voice. He was an activist on behalf of the African American community, who was known for his public unashamed charges against white America and its horrible treatment to the African American community. Those pushing to create diversion would often say that he was advocating racism and violent protest, but this was not the case.

Malcolm X's no nonsense unafraid approach was intimidating to those that felt like the African American community could not and should not have had any power over anyone including themselves. Yet, he pushed on with his message. As a "black Muslim," he was very aggressive and sometimes driven with untamed anger, but he would later take a trip to Africa that would convert him to Sunni Islam. His message of equality and justice would stay the same, but his method would change. Malcolm X was able to bring change and leave a mark on America as a whole but would end up suffering the same fate of previously mentioned young fathers. At the age of 39, he was gunned down by members of the Nation of Islam who were believed to have been paid to murder him in what appeared to be another conspiracy that included members of white America.

In spite of his effectiveness in both life and death, the plague of the lost son still loomed over his legacy. Malcolm X died without a son to continue his passionate fight and be "The Son" the community could look to. Oddly enough, Malcolm X did have a daughter named Qubilah that had a son by the name of Malcolm Shabazz. Malcolm Shabazz's early life resembled that of his grandfather's in that he was a rather troublesome plagued child. He would eventually turn his life around and set out to steer the sons of the African American community in the right direction, citing the fact that there was a hidden agenda for the sons of the black community to be marginalized and placed in correctional facilities. However, in 2013 while in Mexico City, Mexico, Malcolm Shabazz was beaten severely and left stranded to die. He was visiting a Mexican Labor activist who had been deported from the United States in 2013. Detectives believed that it was a robbery gone badly, but many believe that word got around to men who had been following him. Although he was not the immediate son of Malcolm X, his potential to be the voice of a descendent from Malcolm X was enough to warrant "The Lost Son" plague over his life.

Another giant of a name among the list of young fathers the community has had to bury is the Reverend Dr. Martin Luther King Jr. Dr King, like President John F. Kennedy and Malcolm X, was a man whose name will forever ring throughout the ages, just like his somber yet hopeful cries for freedom, peace, and equality. He was a young father whose purpose was not relegated to the pulpit, but instead fashioned for the nation that would need to hear that violence was not the only persuasive tool to be used in destroying the less powerful villain of inequality. Dr. King would come and show the African American community that resistance was just as powerful as violence. He showed the community that

> **Dr. King would come and show the African American community that resistance was just as powerful as violence.**

there was more power in a stance than there was in a fist. As a result, he was revered by the African American community and those that shared the same desire for the community, but he was hated by those who abhorred the ascent of the community to a position of equality. He was jailed, taunted, beaten, humiliated and mocked silently, yet aggressively, while he tore away at the less powerful villain known as segregation. He was successful in getting the victory over segregation, but even he could not escape the fight without losing his life. On April 4, 1968, Dr. King, like JFK and Malcolm X, was assassinated.

Strangely, both Malcolm X and Dr. King were assassinated at the age of 39. Isn't it ironic that a generation is 40 years? It was as though these valiant leaders, who did not live to see age 40, were robbed of their opportunity to usher in the next generation.

After the untimely death of Dr. King, the community was left, yet again, to bury another one of its brave young fathers. Unlike Malcolm X, Dr. King did have sons. However, his two sons would not be the noted fiery sons that the community could look to in place of their valiant father. Martin Luther King III would come on the scene as a son with a desire to fight the less powerful villains that remained but would not exemplify the same burning, unwavering, outspoken, resistant compassion of Dr. King Jr. Martin Luther King III is an advocate for African American rights, but Dr. King was an activist. His second son, Dexter Scott King, would live to manifest a different life purpose, pursuing the true assassins of Dr. King and exposing the conspiracy surrounding his father's assassination. But surprisingly, it was the daughter of MLK, Jr. who dared to pick up her father's mantle lightly touched by her brothers. Though Bernice King, in the image of her father, has won the hearts of

> **It is incumbent upon each of us to carry on the torch of heroism.**

many with her passion, will and determination, society still hopes that either one of her brothers, the male seed, will come forth with full force in the unbridled strength of their father.

Like the sons of the aforementioned heroes, many more have been silenced by death, intimidation, scandal, or simply an unwillingness to embrace the legacies of their fathers. In lieu of this calamity, there is left a burden that lies on not only these lost sons, but also all of humanity. It is incumbent upon each of us to carry on the torch of heroism. We must seek to invent, to discover, to defend, to uphold, and to ignite, building upon the foundations that valiant fathers have laid. Only then will we fulfill God's mandate to be fruitful, multiply, and replenish the earth.

PART TWO

THE PROBLEM

CHAPTER 5

The Reality

The concept in this book deals with the supposition that if Barack Obama had been the father of boys along with girls, America would not have so willingly accepted him. Even though our culture has evolved in many areas, antiquated ideas and entrenched fears still exist that keep us from progressing as a nation. It should not have taken over two hundred years for a black man to be elected President of the United States of America, when other countries have shown progression for many years in their election of minorities and women for powerful positions. But in our country – the land of the free, the melting pot, the coveted place of civil liberties – there is an underlying strength that forbids the real strength of unity, togetherness, and power.

Racism is not the only issue. But because it's so prevalent in our nation, it must become a central part of any conversation that discusses America's thorn. Racism is like a disease that manifests in a body that has a poor hormonal balance. Most people see disease as the problem, but, despite lifestyle and genetics, certain diseases don't exist in perfectly balanced bodies. But the mere fact that the disease exists reveals the underlying problem – hormonal imbalance. So, to diagnose the disease is to realize the root cause. Therefore, in this book I must pause to evaluate the aspect of racism and its correlation to America's lost sons.

There was a television commercial that portrayed a Caucasian mother at the park with her young daughter. The young girl was having the time of her life just playing with a little black girl. Her mother then walked up to her and asked, "Wouldn't you rather play with the other kids, Sweetie?" Innocently, her daughter looked up at her and asked, "Why, Mommy?" Turns out, those "other children" were Caucasian as well. With no answer, the mother stared back in embarrassment and conviction, not having known that the two young girls were classmates. Neither did the mother realize that she had permanently destroyed the fantasy of a non-prejudiced world that only existed in the classrooms of young children.

If you have not noticed, children have no problem at all getting along with one another.

If you have not noticed, children have no problem at all getting along with one another. They can play, read, write, and learn with each other without any apprehension. They only recognize whether a person is mean or friendly; in other words, children pay attention to each other's heart. They have not yet been poisoned with the permanent ink of color. That young girl will be stung by curiosity until she finds out for herself why her mother did not want her to play with the little black girl, thus beginning the never-ending lesson of skin color.

This book exposes the perpetual practice of a racial divide in our communities, which is only allowed to live because of ignorance. Yes, some of the smartest people in the world are the most ignorant. You see, the word ignorant comes from the word ignore, which is what so many have done in America–discredit the value of others who may be different. Most choose to ignore the simple question that the little girl asked her mother: "Why?"

This book exposes the perpetual practice of a racial divide in our communities, which is only allowed to live because of ignorance.

Some may wonder: Why in the world can I not have the same position as a young Caucasian man my age? Why can't I drive the same type of car without being racially profiled? Why am I considered a threat on every street except Wall Street? Many choose not to accept the fact that there is no logical answer. They accept the status quo, simply because it has been the prevailing norms and traditional standards that have been imposed upon them. But it is time to build a new foundation upon this land. It is time to build a foundation that is based upon the colors of men's hearts and not their skin.

As I embarked upon my first few weeks at Morehouse College, my first thought was that I was around too many black people. For my entire life, I had been attending schools that were multicultural and diversified to the utmost. It became awkward for me to be in a place where everybody that surrounded me shared my skin color. It was not just at my school alone, but the two other neighboring colleges are predominately black as well. During high school I was very aware that racism existed, but it was not until college that I realized that a person is not born a racist; racism has to be instilled. Although racism is systemic and taught, truth and innocence are born in delivery rooms every day. The earlier truth is lied to, the less likely chance it has for survival.

Although racism is systemic and taught, truth and innocence are born in delivery rooms every day.

Attending Morehouse was never a dream that I sought to achieve in life. Moreover, I had no idea that I needed to experience some firsthand incidents involving my race in Atlanta in order to awaken some hidden realities of the world I live in. Perhaps, I had been sheltered from this social debacle for so long that I almost forgot of its existence.

But at "The House," there is a daily awakening to who you are regardless of who you become.

Every day, I am surrounded by other aspiring, intellectual young black men who choose to sit in the front of the class, whereas in high school I often chose to sit in the back of class with others who looked like me–not because the teachers made us sit there, but because that was where we were used to sitting and were comfortable with. As a matter of fact, most teachers did not even encourage us to move up close; they only made us sit up front in acts of discipline. Now, I choose to sit upfront at Morehouse because I realize what is behind me. Just a small instance, such as my placement in the classroom, allowed me to become conscious that I do not have to remain where the mindset of America is. It is time now to once and for all diminish the outdated, outworn lesson of racism.

It is amazing how there is still such a racial divide even on Sundays, which should be the day everyone is taught to love others as themselves. But it is the most divided day of the week. It's the time when congregants of like faith come together to reverence whatever divine power they serve. It's one of the few times when diverse members of a family unit can be found all in one place, under one roof. It's a time when love, faith, hope, unity and peace are preached with dynamic fervor. It's a time considered to be the most sacred of all times, yet Sunday is still the most segregated day of the week.

As a "preachers kid," I've often wondered how we got here. Why in a city the size of Memphis and other metropolises aren't there more churches in which parishioners of various skin colors and ethnicities line up to fill the auditoriums? Why is it that the churches that happen to be interracial are usually led by white pastors? As I pondered these thoughts, I was reminded of events in history that might give some insight.

I read about "Bloody Sunday," which occurred on March 7, 1965, in Selma, Alabama. On that day, there was to be a march led by the Southern Christian Leadership Conference (SCLC), where a group of about 600 people attempted to go from Selma to the state capitol in Montgomery to protest Selma's consistent denial of black voting rights. The march was unopposed until the marchers crossed the Edmund Pettus Bridge into Montgomery, where they encountered violent resistance from law enforcers. They were told that the march was illegal and warned that they should turn back into Selma, an episode typical of that movement. But I found one thing thought provoking. Alabama officials gave a direct order to the marchers: "You can go home or you can go to your churches, but you cannot continue this march!" (Sixties).

The marchers were given limited options: home or church. As I expressed in a previous chapter, there's an allotted measure of power assigned to certain individuals, groups, or families by certain other individuals, groups, or families. To be specific, black minorities in America have been subjugated throughout history – forced to stay within superimposed lines. The very thought of a black man exercising power anywhere but within the confines of his own household or inside the four walls of the black church makes some uncomfortable. It's a concept that goes back as far as slavery – when balconies separated the whites from the blacks, who were welcomed to listen to the sermon but were forbidden from operating in any leadership capacity.

My dad was once asked to respond to an article regarding the racial divide in the churches in Memphis, Tennessee, because Memphis was the city where Martin Luther King, Jr. had been assassinated. The publication was a nationally white-owned Christian magazine. When my father responded to the article, where he and other white pastors were asked to contribute opinions, he had to demand that the publishers do a reprint and add his full response as they did the white pastors. For, the magazine reported all of the white pastors' responses in their entirety but only bits and pieces of my father's. The reason for this act was that they did not want the truth to be revealed. (My father's outreach ministry that appears on television and radio, for goodness sakes, is called Touched by the Truth.) What my father said to the magazine was that black people had no problem integrating. "We will drive miles to go to church, whereas white people tend to go to churches near where they live." He also noted that in most cases, but not all, the few disproportionate white families that faithfully attend black churches usually are a part of our staff or our abusive behavior programs. Others are

71

often involved in an interracial relationship or have an interracial child.

The whole notion of the Sunday divide was birthed from slavery when blacks were not allowed in the white churches. Historically, if a white congregation became overpopulated by African Americans, their church either ceased or regrouped and moved elsewhere. In our day, white churches are fine, it seems, with a few black families, but many still won't tolerate an influx. Even mega ministry pastors, like Bishop T.D. Jakes in Dallas; Bishop Charles Blake in Los Angeles; and Pastor Creflo Dollar in College Park, Georgia, whose churches are considered some of the leading African American ministries in America, have a very disproportioned racial balance on Sunday mornings.

> **The ever-present Sunday morning divide has always been a constant reminder of the problem that exists in this country.**

Most times, white Americans consider their attendance to a black church a mission; but when blacks attend their churches, it's considered an upgrade. I believe that people should be able to worship where they wish, as well as where they feel the most comfortable, but I am amazed at the willingness of black Americans to attend white led churches when drastically few white Americans will submit to a predominately black led church. The issue is not that white America does not enjoy our teachers. I know they do. They certainly enjoy our music, but they can't explain their association to their families or their social worlds.

I don't believe that the Sunday divide and the racial divide in America are independent of one another. As a matter of fact, I strongly believe that the former is a direct product of the latter. Unlike the racial tension that developed in Ferguson, Missouri, in August 2014 or that of Sanford, Florida, after the troubling George Zimmerman verdict in July 2013, during times of calm the racial divide in America seems nearly nonexistent. However, the ever-present Sunday morning divide has always been a constant reminder of the problem that exists in this country.

I read an article by Derwin Gray that addressed this concept on the flipside. The author theorized that resolving the Sunday divide could possibly put an end to racism in America:

> "What if black and white evangelicals attended multi-ethnic churches instead of segregated ones? If this Christ-exalting life were to become our reality, we could address racism, oppression, and injustice together. What if black and white evangelicals and other evangelical ethnicities shared life with each other in a local church community and heard each other's stories and walked in each other's shoes? If this Christ-exalting life were to become our reality, I believe our suspicions and mistrust of one another would be

abandoned and replaced with love for one another" ("#Ferguson").

A problem unaddressed can never be solved, and in many cases most interracial congregations seem to act as though there is no problem for fear of offending one another. Therefore, mixed-culture churches don't tend to address publicly the racial problems we see every day. The black church has been known for using its church to rally around certain issues of its hurting communities. Truthfully, that is an aspect of the black community we cannot afford to lose.

My father, Bishop Brandon B. Porter Sr., shared with me that the black church is policed by various special interest groups, more than any other religious organizations, to ensure that certain political advances are no longer projected. Policing is done by threatening the removal of tax exempt status, because the system knows that the African American church in its purest sense has been a major platform to promote the awareness of equality in the United States and the lack of it. When white congregations take a flight out of our communities, we have to remain and strengthen the core, or else there is nothing left to save.

While I believe that there is a need for the black church to keep its identity within the black community, I recognize that the need is greater because of the overwhelming presence of segregation within American culture. Yet again, we must not ignore certain topics when we examine a subject that deals with the African American experience, in this case the plight of black sons. Therefore, in order to bring into this conversation a very vital component relating to lost sons, I thought it expedient to include, along with this one, the subsequent chapters on racism in America.

CHAPTER 6

Judicial Imbalance

W hen America's founding fathers drafted the Constitution, they did so with the intent of securing liberty and justice for every American citizen, not only for those that were alive during that time in 1787, but also, according to its Preamble, for themselves and their posterity. The key word is justice, which can be defined as fair treatment specifically in matters concerning the law. With the adaptation of the Fourteenth Amendment in 1868, African Americans became equal citizens and thereby granted the same rights, privileges, and pursuit of happiness as any other American citizen. But there seems to prevail a certain judicial imbalance in American society that disallows the effectiveness of what those forefathers put in place.

While in the process of writing this book, I was startled by disturbing events that unfolded right in the heart of our country. In Ferguson, Missouri, a suburb of St. Louis, Michael Brown, an 18-year-old African American male, was walking down the street with a friend when he was fatally gunned down by a local police officer. The fact that Brown was shot multiple times while unarmed with his hands raised in surrender stirred up anger not only in that community, but also throughout the nation. The small suburb of Ferguson subsequently erupted into a chaotic frenzy complete with looting, turbulent protests, and violent reactions from the city's police department. As these events captured the nation's attention, the media began to look into the demographics of this small town and the dynamics by which it operates. The Thursday, August 14, issue of USA Today reported the startling statistics that were found: stops by police in Ferguson, Missouri, 4,632 blacks to 686 whites; searches, 562 blacks to 47 whites; arrests, 483 blacks to 36 whites. There's clearly a judicial imbalance in this St. Louis suburb where, according the USA Today, African

> **The fact that Brown was shot multiple times while unarmed with his hands raised in surrender stirred up anger...**

Americans make up two-thirds of the population while, interestingly, the law enforcement in that town is over 90% white (Alcindor).

On a sidebar note, there seemed to have been mixed emotions by some because of the protesting of the local law enforcement officers in that area. Some went so far as to ask, "What about the Black on Black crime?" My answer is that drug dealers and gang members are not on America's taxpayers' payroll; therefore, though the black-on-black element is a serious issue, it is not THE issue as it relates to trained law enforcement officers who are to protect, serve and uphold the law. Accountability is absolutely necessary!

It seems obvious that black men have become casualties in this unspoken and ongoing judicial war.

As I weigh the plight of the black male against that of any other race or gender in America, I find that the scales do not tip in our favor when it comes to justice and equality. For example, black men are sent to prison at alarming rates compared to other races. According to the Bureau of Statistics, one in three black men will go to prison in their lifetime. But is this justified in comparison to the one in seventeen white males that will go to prison? It seems obvious that black men have become casualties in this unspoken and ongoing judicial war. From the retraction of laws regarding the usage and distribution of marijuana to racial profiling and wrongful deaths, our young black men are the target of a discriminatory, unlawful system.

One of the greatest examples of the imbalance of justice can be witnessed through the legalization of marijuana in America. Possession of marijuana is an offense punishable by up to three years in jail. The sale of the drug could lead to a lengthy prison stay, from five years to a life sentence. The alarming fact is that black men are almost 10 times more likely to be arrested for possession of marijuana than white men, and often the black men who are convicted of the crime serve stiffer sentences than their white counterparts.

> **Unfortunately, subsequent to being arrested, imprisoned, and branded with a criminal record, our young black men are being locked into a second-class status...**

With the legalization of marijuana in some states, black men with prior convictions do not have the opportunity to plead their case, which is now justifiable by law. Thousands of black men and boys whose error possibly stemmed from an attempt to provide for their families presently sit and will remain in prisons for possession of a plant that is extremely likely to make others rich. These young black men – often the main target of being searched, frisked and downright disturbed by law enforcement and most times hit with possession of marijuana – aren't even old enough to vote. Now their futures are tainted with prison time and drug offenses behind their names. Unfortunately, subsequent to being arrested, imprisoned, and branded with a criminal record, our young black men are being locked into a second-class status, which often prohibits their voice and their ability to aspire for greatness.

Please don't get me wrong. In no way do I condone criminal behavior. I feel privileged to have been brought up in a two-parent home with a loving, nurturing mother and a hard-working, didactic father who constantly reminded my brother and me of the importance of embracing success. Still, as I gaze upon others who are lacking a positive role model in a struggling economy, I can't help but to sympathize with them and try to make sense of their dilemmas. Yes, they may look like me, but because they grew up without their fathers in their lives, they are not as fortunate as I was; therefore, they were left to rely on their own survival instincts.

As I see it, many young imprisoned black men were victims of desperation – considering having a roof over their heads and feeding their families more important than staying out of trouble. Many of those would-be productive members of society were caught up in a system where drugs, alcohol, sex and money are glamorized and marketed specifically to young black males to eventually set them up for failure. Just like a sniper uses precision and perfect timing to connect his weapon to his victim, these distractions are set up to cause young black men to succumb. The drugs are almost placed in their hands on purpose, and because some believe selling drugs is their only way out of the hood, or it's the road to the fast life, they accept their ultimate demise. Misled to believe that in the course of

As a result of the social oppression that has been placed on them, many young African American males must inwardly struggle to keep from becoming the next statistic.

time they will be able to overcome the stigmas attached to their offense, many young black men fall prey to the deception. Further distracted by society's distrust, these victimized individuals feel the need to prove themselves, not realizing that they were targeted from inception and strategically structured to be defeated.

As a result of the social oppression that has been placed on them, many young African American males must inwardly struggle to keep from becoming the next statistic. For, once seduced by falsely enhanced drugs, alcohol, and illicit sex, they become addicted. The moment they are introduced to the fast life and big money, they become attached to the lifestyle of living lavishly and above their means. Many of them seem to want the newest things but possess the same old mentality. They are made to believe that this false sense of security is the only way of life and that working hard to attain goals is a waste of time, not realizing that this thought is a perception based on lies that have been implanted in their psyche. What was on display for them as a dream, in most cases, becomes a nightmare.

The system I just described illuminates the disappearance and/or displacement of many of America's black sons. Distractions and deception leave them displaced physically, mentally, and emotionally. They are encapsulated in a struggle to find their lost and stolen identity. They are physically locked in prisons, unable to attend college or marry and have a family; and, upon release, powerless to rise above their tainted reputations to try to better themselves. Moreover, when these young men attempt to apply for a job, they are discriminated against as they are often forced to recite their criminal record. They are mentally locked in prisons, left without the mental capacity to overcome the fear of failure, not having the ability to gain integrity because they were checked on the list as "just another black boy." Those newly released from the penal system will usually have minimal resources to help them succeed. They are emotionally displaced as well because they are unable to become the heads of their households. Furthermore, in the cases of those who have sons, there remains a likelihood that the crude, vicious cycle will start again.

CHAPTER 7

The Disenfranchised Son

One of the effects of racism and injustice can be seen through the failure of young black men in America to thrive or come forth. I applaud those who have been able to tunnel through the mountain of inequality and find their path to success. I think it is honorable when a person is able to beat the odds, become established, and leave a legacy for his children. That is why I believe it is so important for us to have Barack Obama in the White House at this time in the life of our country; his election marked a major milestone for black sons in America.

It is time to turn the pages on what has hindered us from coming forth, but we have to acknowledge our issues so that we won't be destined to repeat them. The reality is that years of oppression and the residue that remains in our culture have indeed held back black Americans for decades. Though my generation seems oblivious to it, my grandfather, as well as my father in his youth, witnessed firsthand the struggle of African Americans in their quest for equality. To simply rehearse what can be considered the climax of the historic Civil Rights Movement is to understand and to sympathize with the plight of black America. Take a quick peruse with me as we review our history:

> It is time to turn the pages on what has hindered us from coming forth, but we have to acknowledge our issues so that we won't be destined to repeat them.

On August 28, 1963, 100 years after the executive order of the Emancipation Proclamation, Dr. Martin Luther King Jr. helped to organize a March on Washington for racial equality. On this day in the nation's capital, over 200,000 people stood together to show their opposition to America's economic racism. Included in the crowd was a conglomeration of businessmen and family men of diversity. In many ways, this day could have been seen as a family meeting or a family reunion that was designed to reaffirm and recommit to a promise made of equality 100 years prior. The purpose of this gathering was to enfranchise a people who had been disenfranchised primarily because of their differences in color. For decades, black Americans had been alienated from the possibility of a peaceful citizenship in this great place called America…even while carrying a "promissory note" that stated otherwise.

However, after standing in the long line of the bank of justice in America, some would believe that the promissory note had still not been honored to its fullest. Echoing the sentiments of Dr. Martin Luther King, Jr., America had given its black citizens a "bad check," a check which came back marked "insufficient funds." As a result of this bad check, blacks were held back and in some cases excluded from that which was qualified to be labeled as equality. Consequently, America's black sons were in many ways forced into a mode of life that caused them to accept adaptation rather than to embrace the notion that they too were equal in every aspect of human rights.

Many people will remember the famous "I Have a Dream" ending and how Dr. King so eloquently formulated the argument of America's failure to honor its Declaration of Independence and Constitution:

"In a sense, we have come here to our nation's capital to cash a check. When the architects of our republic wrote the magnificent words of the Constitution and the Declaration of Independence, they were signing a promissory note to which every American was to fall heir. This note was a promise that all men, yes, black men as well as white men, would be guaranteed the unalienable rights of life, liberty, and the pursuit of happiness.

It is obvious today that America has defaulted on this promissory note insofar as her citizens of color are concerned. Instead of honoring this sacred obligation, America has given the Negro people a bad check; a check which has come back marked "Insufficient Funds." But we refuse to believe that the bank of justice is bankrupt. We refuse to believe that there are insufficient funds in the great vaults of opportunity of this nation. So we have come to cash this check; a check that will give us, upon demand, the riches of freedom and the security and justice."   -Dr. Martin Luther King, Jr.

The struggle of America's black sons in cashing the promissory note of justice was fought with difficulty and great struggle. Within the African American leadership was the eagerness to plot a successful course forward. Militants, passives, and non-violent members did everything in their power to show outwardly that they were not pleased with what was being handed down through congressional leaders. However, they inwardly complied, without protest, with the presidential administration in order to force their hand and strike their interest to act on their concerns. Instead of America's bad check providing adequate employment opportunities and middle class upward mobility, it created a lockout in technological advancement and community and economic development symmetry primarily with white suburbs.

Unfortunately, as a result of the bad check written then, its effects are still felt now in that, we yet lack in areas of corporate promotion, social sensitivity, and military and racial equality. The insufficient funds have created a divide in neighborhoods; they've opened up the drug culture in its urban cities, built prisons in rural communities, and began a systemic emasculation of the black male physique, pitting the black man and black woman against each other and taking out those essential and pivotal elements that make up the black family.

Moreover, the rate of black unemployment has been twice that of whites since the March on Washington. Black unemployment for the last few years has been more than the annual average national percentage rate of the recession years since 1963 (Fletcher). A lack of economic freedom, financial literacy, access to capital, and political agenda or representation has come short of legislatively making the black community whole.

For the last 50 years, it would seem as if blacks have always faced severe employment issues, and when compared to the entire labor market, it's as though blacks would statistically be in a perpetual recession. If one were to pay close attention to the appearance of things, it would appear to be that the economic disparity is the plot of a less diversified government of conservatives who would prefer a diminished human worth community that will forever be dependent on its government for wealth creation. One could assume that blacks remain taken advantage of by whites who claim, often falsely, to represent their interest as they are used to bolster democratic values.

Whether one is a Democrat or Republican, the insufficient check, spoken about by Dr. King, has imposed what is almost an irreparable harm on the opportunity for the black sons of America to advance politically, socially, morally, academically, domestically, globally, and/or personally. When there is dysfunction in what is known to be a necessary cell in the family unit, black sons are more prone to live in penitentiaries rather than on the campus of universities. So where are America's black sons? The answer is disproportionately IN JAIL– compared to those in the White House, the Pentagon, or Wall Street. With a majority of the African American males carrying some correctional history and while more under employed or non-employed blacks sons are separated from their children having dropped out of high school with no prospects of secondary or post graduate achievements, black sons in America still appear to be destined to lag behind in any achievement gap scenario.

> **In America, power has always been the possession of the elite and usually well preserved and never shared.**

In America, power has always been the possession of the elite and usually well preserved and never shared. The old adage, quoted by John Emerich Edward Dalberg Acton, "Power tends to corrupt, and absolute power corrupts absolutely," is very appropriate for the present conversation regarding America and its black sons. As of today, there is little, if any, knowledge of an institution within American society dedicated to dispensing reparations that would even the playing field.

Few, if any, programs are available that would close the barn door of misery because of distinction or lessen the insult caused by inhumane treatment of a race of people for hundreds with free labor for infrastructure, industry, domestication, and maturation of America's white society.

Of a truth, the African American race should not be given a check for the many years of experiential disenfranchisement, but instead America should be required to compensate its black sons for the opportunities lost. In every facet of life – socially, morally, legally, personally and generationally – the black community has been infected with a substandard lifestyle in education, access to capital, legal protection, safe neighborhoods, health care, and upward mobility. Because it is not in the interest of America to share legislative and political power with any group other than those who are insulated with it and those who will institutionalize it for posterity, a bad check cannot restore lost opportunity and possibilities.

In a significant moment that will go down in history, America decided to turn its bad check into a poker chip and bet on black.

As previously mentioned, all good things must come to an end. The recession of 2007 had America in a face off with a global economic meltdown which had never been witnessed since the Great Depression. As a result of the Great Recession, the economic survivability of not only the US, but also the world as we knew it was threatened. Economist predicted massive workforce reductions, stockpiles of cash, and average workers hitting the street like rain drops in a summer storm. All hope of instant recovery in order to save a Presidential election was waning. Republicans recruited a Wall Streeter to carry their message, and Main Street

(Democrats) picked a community organizer from the rough side of Chicago. America was enraged about the bailout strategy for the rich that in all actuality left out the poor. In a significant moment that will go down in history, America decided to turn its bad check into a poker chip and bet on black.

This move would take a black son whose disenfranchisement had no bearings on his enlightenment to the limitless possibilities he possessed as a son of America, whether black or white, rich or poor. The historic election of President Barack Obama was in so many ways the nation signaling a deep departure from an old mentality. The new mentality accepted the truth that America's black sons possessed more than the strength to plow a field and endure hardship but that they possessed the mental capacity to lead a country that had been deemed the most powerful country in the world.

However, there was still another assumption. There was still the assumption that maybe he was bet on by some to be a scapegoat for the next four years without the intention of eight years. Nevertheless, the truth stands unmoved and unmovable, that a black son tunneled through the mountains of racial inequality, left the bad check of injustice at the bank of America, and reached beyond the limitations of an inherited disenfranchisement to sit at the head of a nation whose feet had for so long remained on the head of its black sons.

The historic election of President Barack Obama was in so many ways the nation signaling a deep departure from an old mentality.

CHAPTER 8

Political Unrest

In the spring of 2008, a sixty-five year old African American grandmother was sitting at her dinner table with her five adult children discussing the upcoming election. "It's a strong possibility that he might win," one of them told her in order to convince her that she should go to the polls in support of the first black man to be a viable contender in the race for President of the United States. But despite the country's overwhelming enthusiasm and the compelling of her children, the grandmother made a bold confession: "I won't vote for Barack Obama. I don't want him to win. If he wins, 'they' might assassinate him."

Unlike her children who were in their early forties and were only babies during the Civil Rights Movement of the sixties, the grandmother could vividly remember sitting in front of the old black and white television set or listening to the dusty, staticky radio when the news reporters would sadly announce that the "President has just been shot,"... that "Martin Luther King was assassinated today,"... that "Senator Robert Kennedy is dead." She shared the sentiment of perhaps a handful of incredulous African Americans who would rather see black America lose this election than to witness what they thought might be another inevitable tragedy.

Needless to say, several years later and despite those odds, the twice elected President Barack Obama has survived the physical threat of being the first black man in the White House. In the middle of his second term, however, it seems that the grandmother's premonition is coming to pass in the egregious, unprovoked character assassination of our current Unites States President. It's as though some politicians want him to figuratively die in office by attacking his good intentions

> **In lieu of events surrounding our political scenes, it appears that the politics get muddier and muddier as we progress toward the coming election.**

with their threatening of lawsuits and impeachment in an effort to kill his political influence.

In lieu of events surrounding our political scenes, it appears that the politics get muddier and muddier as we progress toward the coming election. The statement that I am about to make is not biased nor slanted toward any particular party, but as I was watching Fox News looking for some of the current issues surrounding our world, I could only hear derogatory, disrespectful remarks about our President. I watched in amazement at how it seems our world has become so overt with unbridled character assassinations of world leaders. Even during the Civil Rights Movement of old, the participating activists were at least respectful in their disagreement or opposition to leaders' actions or decisions.

To say that Barack Obama is incompetent is a blatant misjudgment of an accomplished leader. Even to stand on the floor in the Senate or Congress and openly interrupt the President of the United States and say that he's a liar is not something any other President would have had to endure, even though we know that all of them may have lied. My reason for inserting this thought or observation is that I believe we are seeing what I call "blackophobia," similar to the accepted theory of homophobia. Blackophobia is the fear of the rise of black successful leadership.

Say what you will, but there is still a problem in America. And it's not whether you are liberal or conservative. The issue sadly enough is still color. Trust me. I am not making excuses about the struggle of black people or our need for white people to give us their space. All I ask is to let us in the race.

How much do we have to do to prove our competence? One serves two terms in the White House as

President and doesn't know anything? Really? Whether people admit it or not, President Barack Obama, his amazing wife, and beautiful daughters have proven the ability of Black America to handle the highest seats of honor in America. I believe that there are those who want to paint this administration in a cynical fashion only to deter the future plights of young black men and women. And if Barack Obama indeed had a son, in my opinion, there would be a deeper agenda of the naysayers. I have no hate for any race of people. I am just stating the facts of some and their behaviors as it relates to a black presence in the White House.

Segregation is still real – maybe not on the signs at the water fountains, movie theaters, restaurants, or public restrooms – but it exists in the hearts of men. I must pause to give our country an A for effort, though. Lawmakers have tried and are still trying to get away from the stigma attached to decades of Jim Crow. For the most part, African Americans have been included on almost every level – as integral members of the social, religious, educational, and political sectors of society. But within each of those arenas there exists a surreptitious minority whose purpose is to sabotage justice and perpetuate the idea that blacks and whites are unequal. I thank God that racism

98

is not in all men's hearts, but I must express that there is still wickedness in high places.

So what's the purpose of this conversation? In a nutshell, the purpose is to expose to the coming generations the eroding hearts of many of our parents because there is prejudice of every kind. Most of us will agree that prejudice is taught behavior, passed down from generation to generation. To conquer an engrafted mindset, we must seek to learn more about one another and how similar our differences really are. Most people think that the less you know about people, the easier it is to love them, but not so. The more you know about people, the more you find out we are not that different. It's true that people are destroyed for a lack of knowledge, but people also destroy because of a lack of knowledge! So then, education is the key to understanding. If there is no education, there can be no change in anyone's understanding. Get this: the understanding is what we have been *standing under*, but education helps us to move on to better perspectives in life.

> **If there is no education, there can be no change in anyone's understanding.**

Every human is entitled to his or her preference, but not to the point that one shackles or prohibits another from constitutional rights and opportunities for success. We have seen a lot of changes in recent years within our nation, and these historic changes take place no matter the resident political party. Yes, change is inevitable. However, choice is still allowed in our democratic society.

Whether liberal or conservative, religious or nonreligious, people have the right to choose, and then they have the responsibility to live with the consequences of their choices. All of us have that right on Election Day, and if by chance our choice does not win, we should still pray for the success of the nation. Isn't it amazing how in the time of crisis the real strength of unity and brotherhood that this nation was built upon comes to the forefront? For instance, subsequent to the tragic events of 9/11, when America experienced the worst terroristic attack in its history, all Americans stood together to fight against the evil that sought to destroy our country. Those were colorless moments because America was covered with the debris of fear, anxiety, and rescue. It did not matter his or her affiliation, race, religion, or political party, every American citizen stood as one; praying the same prayer; seeking the same justice; shedding the same tears. During that bleak, somber time in America's history, we became as one. This unity was unquestioned by our adversaries because the red, white and blue was held up through and through.

> **Whether liberal or conservative, religious or nonreligious, people have the right to choose, and then they have the responsibility to live with the consequences of their choices.**

Remember: One nation under God with liberty and justice for all! A house divided against itself will not stand...even if it's the House of Representatives.

PART THREE

THE REMEDY

CHAPTER 9

The Urgency of Time

I would be remiss if I did not address the crucial topic of time in this dissertation. This concept is imperative because, if not taken seriously, we will reach a level of extinction. We must strive to preserve our leaders: our activists, educators, entrepreneurs, doctors, civic leaders and, I dare even say, politicians within this great nation. If we want to begin strengthening those who hold these positions, as well as preparing the next generation of those who will fill them, we must begin now.

In today's generation we seem to mistake time for a stopwatch – something we can stop at the click of our thumb. We often tend to procrastinate and focus on trivial matters instead of handling our primary responsibilities. Time truthfully waits for no one, but some people wait to begin chasing their dreams as if it does. Every day that we wake up and take a fresh breath of air, time passes us by. It is essential that we make proper use of time throughout the course of our day because we can never get it back. The swiftness of time should encourage the urgency to accomplish our goals while we maintain an ambitious mindset.

There seems to be a horrible epidemic going around that deals with waiting until a certain age to make a difference in society. Now is the time to begin proving others wrong about this generation. There is no need to wait until you are turning gray to make a difference in someone's life or to change the world around you. If you want to be a doctor, you can start preparing for that now. Even after a college class, you can take the initiative to do more research than what is asked of you. If you have an idea that you know could change the perception of the world in a certain area, begin acting on that now. The world is eager for new ideas and easier ways to do things.

> **There seems to be a horrible epidemic going around that deals with waiting until a certain age to make a difference in society.**

Take note of those whose hard work and efficient utilization of time have made life easier for everyone else. Who would have ever thought we would reach a time where people could advertise their business through the click of a mouse, allowing them to expose ideas and network with anyone across the globe? This creation was a result of someone's taking the initiative to spend time thinking of ways to make life easier. It just so happened that the inventor was a 20-year-old from New York named Mark Zuckerberg, who was tired of waiting around for someone to pat him on his back and tell him that he could be a game changer in the technological world. At the age of 28, Mark reached a net worth of over thirteen billion dollars through the creation of his business Facebook, all because he chose to not waste his time.

Taking the time to act now on your dreams will provide you with the opportunity to live in them later. And by later, I do not mean after your sixties, but even before then when you can truly enjoy the sacrifices of your hard work at an early age. There is never a limit on how hard you can work, but there is a limit on how long you can work hard.

I learned a lot about hard work and sacrifice during my middle and high school basketball career. In high school, my coach was adamant about accepting nothing less than perfection. We would have practice at 5:30 in the morning and go to class at 7:00. School was out at 2:00, and immediately at 2:30 we would begin weight training. Following that, practice began again at 4:30 to about 7:00. Through this tough time schedule, my coach stressed personal discipline and time management to enhance our study habits as well as our performance on the court. As a result, I adopted a sickening work ethic and would try my best to go as hard as I could every time I stepped foot onto that court for that limited time of practice. Many times, I became angry with the coach

> Quite honestly, in today's society the more free time you have, the more time you have to lose your freedom.

on his game-time decisions concerning playing time, but I had to learn that part of the privilege of the coach was to select whom he wished, and my privilege was to work hard so that I could perform to the best of my ability whenever I was given the opportunity. In the words of my father, "Life is competitive, but greatness lives through the consistent attribute of self motivation. Life is about more than getting on the team. It's about getting in the game. Favor gets you on the team, but personal performance keeps you in the game!"

Quite honestly, in today's society the more free time you have, the more time you have to lose your freedom. So often, we have young teenagers in this country who are arrested because they have too much time on their hands. Sitting around corner stores all day does nothing to enhance the ideas that you have in your mind that could possibly allow you to own a chain of successful corner stores.

Why can we not use the time we have properly when we have the choice on how to spend it? The more time we choose to lose, the more time we spend in jail cells. The more time we choose to wait, the more dreams we choose to waste. It has to begin now. There is nothing more precious on this earth than time. Lau Tzu said, "The journey of a thousand miles begins with one step." By the time you finish that last mile, however, you do not want to be old and on the decline. So start now!

Time is the most sought after asset known to humanity.

The best way to maximize your time is to learn how to manage it. From the time you wake up until the time you lay your head down to go to sleep at night, your day should be planned out. There should never be a time where you are not being productive in some matter until you are very established in what you want to do. It all stems from the idea that you truly do not have time to lose.

Imagine that while you are sleeping, someone on this earth is getting closer to completing your dream than you are. Someone is outworking you to get that spot on the team. Someone is studying harder than you to receive the higher ranking in the class. Someone is getting up at five in the morning and not getting home until six in the evening. Why? Because he or she understands that time well spent is more valuable than time well rested. I'm not insinuating that sleep is not good, but rather that sleeping only leads to more dreaming than acting. Sooner or later you will have to awaken and take the challenge.

If time were something we should not worry about, then there would be no watches, clocks, or calendars. Go to any correctional facility around this nation and have the chance to sit and talk one on one with inmates and ask this simple question, "What is one thing you wish you could get back?" I guarantee over ninety percent of them would respond saying, "I wish I could get back the time that I've wasted in here." It took them to be locked up to understand that they took for granted the most sought after asset on this planet, and now rue the fact that they will do time for not managing it.

Some of the most shared conversations among members of retirement facilities deal with some aspect time: the time spent raising their children, the time spent with their spouses or significant others, the time spent in their careers, the time spent enjoying life, etc. Every person has to understand that the day will come when he or she can no longer work, so make the most out of right now while you have the best strength of your entire life.

Time is the most sought after asset known to humanity. We must manage it well so that we won't feel regret when it's almost gone. Understand that anyone can lay his or her head down on a pillow and have a dream, but only greatness will take the time to wake up and act on it.

CHAPTER 10

Under the Hoodie

People often use the metaphorical phrase, "You should never judge a book by its cover," but in today's society, as long as the cover is presentable, anything can reside on the inside.

Separatism has existed in this country for hundreds of years, and quite frankly it has been silently awakened over the course of these past few years. Since when has it become a threat for a young man with a bag of Skittles and a can of tea to walk home in the comfort of his hoodie? Or for someone to turn up his friends' and his favorite song when it comes on the radio in the car? (So much for not judging a book by its cover) Coming from a young teenager raised in Memphis, it seems that if you have on khakis and Cole Haans and run a stop sign, it was an accident; but if you have on jeans and Jordans, you were recklessly driving.

Dallas Maverick owner Mark Cuban stated, "If I see a black kid in a hoodie, and it's late at night, I'm walking to the other side of the street. And if on the other side of the street, there's a guy that has tattoos all over his face – white guy, bald head, tattoos everywhere – I'm walking back to the other side of the street." To me, this statement is just a pure example of the reality of perception. People will always be recognized for what's on the outside, but judged on the inside. The only fault is the reality of perception has made our eyes entirely outweigh our ears in the sense that people always like to see and judge one another instead of taking the time to listen.

I bet if George Zimmerman would have taken the time to simply ask Trayvon Martin where he was going, instead of letting the perception of his eyes think for him, the African American society and even the world could have been spared a devastating travesty. There may come a time when we won't be judged by color or outer appearance; until then we must understand and digest the fact that there is rarely going to be a drive-through set up for our success. We can't just order it and pick it up. We must buy the groceries, wash them, and cook success, teaching our children's children to do the same thing as they live and learn.

While you should never judge a book by its cover, I have never in my lifetime seen or heard of a respected black man in corporate America who sags his pants and uses profanity every three words. It's not enough to want the part. We have to look and sound the part no matter what field we decide to go into.

Only 3.8 % of this country's physicians legally identify themselves as African American (Boukus). Only a half dozen of approximately 1, 900 senators have been black (Holland). Yet, blacks compose nearly 78% of the NBA, and 68% make up the NFL (Sherley). Are the basketball courts and football fields the only places we can avidly strive? Of course not! We just have to be mentally focused and prepared to step out of our comfort zones.

Escaping the captivation of a "hood" mentality will be the starting point of our success, and reaching back to educate while connecting the captivated will be our intended destination. People are so often blinded by the methods of success in the hood to the point where prosperous people in the surrounding *neighborhoods* are looked upon as lames. The most talked about topic in the hood is the subject of leaving, but you can never escape what you choose not to understand. What most people don't understand is that many people in the hood have natural talent and abilities that can be redirected into more positively productive endeavors. For example, the same ingenious, methodical approach used in making and selling illegal drugs can be put into going back to school and obtaining a degree in pharmaceutical studies. The same intellect, energy and hard work that you put into playing sports, you can apply to finding the next breakthrough in sports medicine.

Read the following line very carefully: The only barrier stopping you is the residing pun of your "true face" being hidden under the ignorance and comfort of your hoodie, or environment. This "hood" mentality has been our comfort for so long that we are afraid to be exposed to reality and touched by the failures that allow dreams to become reality. Change never comes without a challenge; therefore, we have to understand that absolutely nothing will be given to us except an occasional handout.

> **The same intellect, energy and hard work that you put into playing sports, you can apply to finding the next breakthrough in sports medicine.**

Going against expectation is one of the hardest tribulations to overcome. Many young blacks are commonly expected to try but rarely expected to conquer. So many times, the existing fear of sacrificing expected success (sports) for obtained success (Masters or Doctorate degrees) is a huge mental hindrance. At any point in time, you can break your knee and end your sports career, but one thing nobody in this world can take from you is knowledge. The key is not becoming comfortable with your failures, but becoming acquainted with learning from them.

Obama made it blatantly clear when he stated that if he had a son, he would look like Trayvon. The President obviously made a strong statement revealing how he felt about the disheartening verdict of the State of Florida vs. George Zimmerman case. The simple judgment of this case should give young black men the burning ambition to want to fill the perspective positions that unconstitutionally bound us. It has clearly been proven that this can be done, seeing that we have a black President. The only problem is that he doesn't have a son to pour into, which is the reason he comes to schools such as Morehouse College in the West End of Atlanta and Booker T. Washington High School in the heart of the hood in Memphis. It is more to his term than just ending world hunger and instituting Obama Care. He has publicly shown that he is here to back us up and push us; the only thing we have to do is be willing to listen and genuinely put forth an honest effort to rising to the occasion. One can never argue with success; therefore, Barack Obama is the ultimate mentor.

Through the absence of a Barack Obama Jr., a nation of young Obamas has been born and taken under the wing of the most powerful man in the world. When President Obama placed his hand on that bible, let the final words of the Presidential oath fall off the tip of his lips into that microphone filling the ears of more than 20 million people, and was inaugurated on January 20, 2009, he took off his "hoodie," put on his tailored suit, and set up an appointment for every young African American man in this nation to get fitted and pick up his own suit as any other father would. Young men (and women), we have to realize that the zipper of the "hoodie" has finally been unzipped in the most powerful way possible. It is time for us to try on other outfits, to change out of the comfort of our fitted jerseys into a fitted suit, to exchange our colorful facemasks for blue doctor's masks, and to button up our dress shirts while unbuttoning our lips.

> **In order to be respected, at some point you have to be heard.**

In order to be respected, at some point you have to be heard. In no shape, form or fashion, should anyone study until his brain is burnt out and never reveal any information that is obtained. God did not give us a mouth to listen; that is why we have ears. But in the natural anatomy of our bodies, from top to bottom, the ears come before the mouth, so we should definitely listen before we speak. Like the old saying goes: closed mouths just simply do not get fed. If ever there is a time to speak, there is a time to listen; and the opportunity to speak will present itself again. We have to know how and when to speak. The First Amendment granted everyone the pleasure of freedom of speech, but the burden of listening is still optional.

Nine times out of ten, if people don't feel as though what you are saying is beneficial in a positive way, they don't want to hear you, and they will shun everything that is being said. In order to get your point across, you must know who is on the other side. You cannot talk to a group of political officials the same way you talk to your best friend or your average acquaintance on the street. This form of

We have the ultimate gate opened for us, and we still want to hop it?

education coincides with metaphorical reference of changing clothes into a suit. We have to become well read as well as well spoken.

We have the ultimate gate opened for us, and we still want to hop it? Is this the moment Dr. King laid in a puddle of blood only a few feet away from the safety of his hotel room for? the moment Rosa parks was stripped of her rights as an intelligent black lady and treated as an Egyptian slave for? the moment our 44th President was born, destined, and "deprived" of a male son for? But for every young child in America that has been deprived of a dad, you now have a father in the White House with your best interest in mind and at heart – someone who finally sits in the "big chair" and understands the struggle of being labeled by not just the clothes that he wears, but the skin that he's in. There is no better time than now for us to change clothes, because no one hops a gate in a suit; you walk through it in one. The thing about a gate, though, is that it doesn't stay open forever. Eventually, at some point, it has to close, and who is to say when it will ever be opened again?

Therefore, we have to allow our minds at this point in history to dream outside of what we are comfortable with. Know that it's okay to wear a hoodie if it describes where you are trying to go. But we have worn this "hoodie" for too long, while fashion trends have been evolving for years upon years. Knowing who we are while accepting the fact that we all have the intellectual capability to be a walking definition of greatness is the epitome of climbing out of our comfort zone. If the United States had become content with just walking around here on earth, we would not have made the astonishing breakthrough of

Know that it's okay to wear a hoodie if it describes where you are trying to go.

exploring outer space and doing what no man is comfortable with – walking on the moon.

Do you think Jackie Robinson was comfortable with being the only African American player in the most popular sport in the country with the chance of his head being caved in dramatically by the emphatic force of a baseball traveling over 85 miles per hour? Of course not! He had to crawl out of his comfort zone for not just himself, but for the integration of sports around the entire world. Consequently, he is still making history in the success of Chicago's Jackie Robinson West Little League Baseball Team, cited as the "pride of Chicago." These 11 and 12 year old African American sons won the US Finals in Pennsylvania, August 2014, giving "the whole city something to cheer about" ("Jackie Robinson West").

Dr. Martin Luther King Jr. and the entire assemblage of civil rights activists were in no way at all comfortable with a plethora of vicious, flesh tearing German Shepherds running towards them from every angle – not at all. They made up in their minds that they wanted to receive equal rights for not only themselves, but also for us, their children's children. And slowly but surely, as they were sprayed down under the impenetrable pressure of fire hoses, they took off the rags that were soaking wet, showered themselves, and began to put on their double-breasted Ralph Lauren suits and customized Donna Karan dresses.

At some point someone else has to take a stand. My only question is, "Why should you be the one who is sitting down?"

CHAPTER 11

Power Prepares Power

It seems as though every day I turn on the television there is always some sort of horrific breaking news about someone abusing power: precious, innocent children that have not even been privileged to reach the age of twelve months old, taken out of the gentle, cradling arms of their parents and slaughtered; or marvelous women that aspire to grace the earth angelically with a strong strut of significance accompanied by an impactful fragrance of positivity, abused and left helpless to lapse in the depression of their own self worth. I attentively shift to the edge of my seat, while my heart sinks into the bottom of my stomach in shock as I watch young men my age as brave young soldiers enter warzones all over the world – sometimes stripped of life in battles with countries whose militia targets the lives of innocent people in a colorless search for the true meaning of their own lives. This greed of power has totally taken a negative turn in the direction of damnation. Power is only positively prevalent where people understand their purpose, but to understand purpose you must have the proper preparation.

President Obama has not always been the most powerful man in the world. He did not by any means just lollygag into the destiny of the magnificent man he is today. Oprah Winfrey did not just wake up and become the most powerful and influential woman on this planet. These two great heroes are also not the first powerful people to walk this earth. They wisely took the initiative to put together the sum total of every powerful person that inspired them before their time, combined with a stringent work effort.

Oprah Winfrey did not just wake up and become the most powerful and influential woman on this planet.

If you want to exceed where most people tarry, you have to exceed what most people know, which takes ceaseless devotion. Your appetite for greatness has to become so strong that you reach the point where you despise the taste of mediocrity. This is the most effective way of preparing for what you have yet to experience; the catch is being able to discipline yourself to handle it. Charles Caleb Colton adequately stated "To know the pains of power, we must go to those who have it…." Every great person to ever live has experienced the taste of immaculate inspiration from someone who preceded him or her.

In modern times we have many cases of this preparation of power. George W. Bush most definitely received inspiration from his father, George H. W. Bush, to become the second President in the Bush family. It is probable thought that President George W. Bush's election was ensured by the fact that his father had previously served a total of twelve years in the White House, proving the theory that power prepares power. This process occurs not just on a political stage, but also from a religious standpoint as well. Joel Osteen, pastor of Lakewood Church in Houston, Texas, now resides over the largest church in the nation. He started out working faithfully within the media ministry serving underneath his father until one day his purpose shook hands with promise and created a supernatural power of positive inspiration that was ready to impact the lives of millions.

It is probable thought that President George W. Bush's election was ensured by the fact that his father had previously served a total of twelve years in the White House...

Barack Obama, as the most powerful man in the world, desires to inspire many to exceed the milestones that he has completed. Take the time to imagine Barack Obama

123

Jr., growing up in the most powerful household in the world for eight years. The simple thought of a young African American boy becoming a man in the White House is quite astounding. Of course, since this scenario is non-existent, President Obama has no choice but to prepare his two daughters and the rest of our generation for the burden of power.

Everyone is born with the strength to obtain power, but select few have the wisdom to handle it properly. The secret to becoming positively powerful is developing the right character, knowing how to communicate, and becoming committed to what some people do not have the courage to stand for, even in the face of death.

Becoming powerful begins with training up the right character to manifest in your life. Inevitably the provision of power will reveal your character. There are absolutely no shades of gray when it comes to the colors of a righteous heart. Your power will either be put towards negativity or positivity, evil or good. Surrounding yourself with people of ill intentions will only result in bad habits. You must not seek to be understood, but seek for a complete understanding. In other words, people will not always smile upon your decision to become set apart from others. Do not become discouraged when people snobbishly murmur that you think you are too good to do what everyone else does, because in all honesty and actuality you are. No one deserves an untrustworthy leader. If a true exemplary character is developed, you will impact lives day by day simply by the morals you exemplify.

Like character, the element of communication will always be considered a key to becoming powerful. During ancient times the words out of a king's mouth created decrees that could change the future of a dynasty forever, for good or for bad. Words can either administer hope or distribute disparity. In fact, words are so powerful that they shape the atmosphere around you.

The atmosphere is made up of atoms, so when you speak positive atoms into the atmosphere, your surroundings will have to be uplifting. Vice versa, if you choose to be pessimistic about everything that comes your way, you will be surrounded by hopelessness. When you allow elements of hope and prosperity to come out of your mouth, you allow faith and strength to fall into the ears and hearts of the hopeless. In fact, words are so powerful that they inevitably bind you. You can never take back what you choose to say, but people will always resort to choosing permanent reactions to the words you only meant

You must be committed like never before in order to become what people have never seen before.

for a temporary moment. You never know a person's situation, so something so miniscule as attacking someone verbally out of anger can cause him or her to commit unjust suicide out of sorrow. The power of life and death is truthfully in the tongue. You should always be quick to listen and slow to speak.

125

Another key to communication is knowing your audience. I cannot relay a message to a 75-year-old the same way I would to a 15-year-old. Being flexible in your method of communication can sometimes be referred to as code switching. Most importantly, the power of communication is about realizing what people want to hear while knowing what people must understand.

Following communication is commitment, which is most certainly a discipline. You must be committed like never before in order to become what people have never seen before. The power of commitment destroys the will of contentment. The harder you work towards obtaining every goal you set out to accomplish, the weaker the habits of failure become in your life. There are twenty-four hours in a day. It is often said that a good night's rest consists of eight hours of sleep, but a great lifetime's rest might consist of only four hours of sleep. If you complete college courses with mediocre study habits, you will continue to receive mediocre results. By pushing the limits and sacrificing time that others use for temporary pleasure, you will exceed limiting expectation.

The difference between a champion and an occasional winner is the power of commitment.

In order to write this book, I had to make some major sacrifices. There were nights where I came home from work around 4:30 in the evening and had to stay up writing

126

until 4:30 in the morning only to wake up at 7:00, but I was committed to finishing. There were times when my friends would all be out partying on the weekends just enjoying being home from school, but I stayed in because I was committed to finishing something that would help them in the long run. I encountered countless nights of unintentionally being up to witness the sunrise of another day, but I was committed to finishing what would be the dawning of a new day for a generation.

Being committed is about facing what others refuse to look at, which in turn causes you to emerge as the leader you were born to be. This goes for any aspect in your life in which you want to see change occur. The difference between a champion and an occasional winner is the power of commitment. Power is there for those who are willing to commit to enduring the challenging endeavors that reveal how to contain it.

When you search for character, you find kindness. When you learn to communicate, you create clarity. And when you agree to becoming committed, you establish courage. Unfortunately, with the gift of power comes the curse of loneliness. Sometimes, you have to walk alone to properly direct the path of many. It will hurt to change your companions to people who are fit for shaping your future, but a poor man cannot tell a rich man how to become successful; he can only tell him what not to do. Yes, it will be difficult to start exchanging a good time for a great book, but only iron sharpens iron. It will be tremendously hard to put down the cup of fear and drink from the fountain of true life, but only power prepares power.

CHAPTER 12

The Investment

I am reminded of a story that was once told about a young lad who was excited to accompany his father to work one day. The entire night before the big day, all the son could talk about was how much fun the two were going to have. The son wanted nothing more in this world than to grow up and be like his favorite superhero, his father. The two had breakfast early that morning, a time full of laughter and joy. Then they headed off to work. When they finally arrived, the son could not wait to get started. After going into the front office to clock in, they got down to business.

As the son sat drawing imaginative pictures of the wonderful day he and his father were about to embark upon, a man walked up to his father and sarcastically commented, "You brought your son in to watch you wipe off dusty desks and filthy tables? What a great dad you are," and walked off. The son thought nothing of it and continued to work on his drawing. A few moments went by, and then a lady walked up to the young boy, squeezed him on the cheek, and said, "Aw, you are too cute to be here handling trash with your daddy." She strutted off. The young boy became curious as to why those two people had insulted his hero but immediately shook the thought and continued sketching. Around ten minutes later, another man walked by and told the boy's father, "Hey, you loser! If you keep missing spots on the floor, I will get you fired in the blink of an eye. Now, get back to work!" and angrily stomped away. The son threw down his paper and crayons; then with tears flooding down his face asked his father, "Daddy, why are they so mean? Why are they making fun of you? Why do you let them treat you this way, Daddy?" The father walked his son to the backroom, got down on one knee, wiped the boy's tears, and said, "Son, I do this so you won't have to. One day when you grow big and strong, you will understand." With tears forming in his eyes, the father

So the son carries out in strength what the father knows in wisdom.

turned around, wiped his face, and then gripped his son in an affectionate hug of comfort like never before.

A father finds strength in his son, and a son seeks the wisdom of his father. Most of the things that fathers wish they could do by the time their sons come of age, they can no longer do because of the natural effects on the human body. So the son carries out in strength what the father knows in wisdom. But this rite of passage does not just come simply by way of an eighteenth birthday, not by any means. It comes after years of efficient training and investing.

I define investing as sacrificing temporary windows of opportunity to open everlasting doors of abundance.

People invest to ensure a surplus in their future. The moment a man becomes a father, his burden and blessing of investing begins. It is no longer about him anymore. It is now about raising someone who will be greater than he but will never let the world forget who invested in him.

Since I am a business finance major in school, I have decided to kill two birds with one stone: give a quick lesson for a course credit in business finance and also break down the process of "namely transitioning." I define investing as sacrificing temporary windows of opportunity to open everlasting doors of abundance. With that being said, there are three types of investments: cash equivalent, lending, and ownership. But unarguably the effects of "insensible inflation" can hinder the process of the transfer of legacy, for investing without adequate training is inevitable abuse.

The first phase of investing we will metaphorically deal with is the cash equivalent stage. When handling cash equivalents, these investments are extremely easy to convert back to cash and often considered one of the safest forms of investing. During the young stages of a son's life, he is put in elementary and middle school to get the basis of his education. Often, small supplements of freedom and fun are granted in this stage. But at any given time that the child gets distracted and falls off track, he can be disciplined and easily placed back on the direction of obedience. Not too much responsibility is given at this point, only a miniscule amount that can result in very inconsequential failures, such as forgetting to do chores or receiving horrible comments from a teacher about class behavior. These actions are often handled by some sort of parental punishment that affirms to the child that in no shape, way, form, or fashion is the act of disobedience acceptable nor will it be tolerated. Immediately, the child is molded back into the rules of the household, simply by the chastising fear of being punished again. Unfortunately, this phase of timidity digresses with age because as the child gets older, the temptation of negative influence gets stronger.

The next step of investing is lending. This investment comes with a slightly higher degree of risk. At this point you are lending money to corporations, the most commonly known might be a bond. And, of course, when you lend something, you expect to receive it back. Metaphorically speaking, the son now has flourished into high school. Growing up, he was pretty disciplined, but now the temptation of negative influence has skyrocketed like a missile destined for the never-ending mysterious boundaries of outer space. By the age of sixteen, driving comes into play and the old-reliable family car is passed down. Driving can now be a privilege or a tragedy. The father lends his car to his son, trusting that he will make the right decisions on his own now that he is maturing; but allowing one wrong person in the car with the possession of drugs can land the young man in a world of trouble, likely resulting in jail time. As time progresses, the parents might take a trip for the weekend out of town. While the mother is slightly nervous for her growing baby boy, the father is trusting, yet testing, him to be the "temporary" man of the house while they are gone. It all goes back to how grounded the son is and whether he shall take the path of being a leader or a follower. Hoping the young man will conquer all of these "tests," the father is one step away from completing his job, and the son is one step away from signing the new contract of owning his family name. The only catch is that the young man can no longer be sheltered. He has to decide to be a man for himself or deal with the pain of not properly handling the most crucial and final deposit of his father's investment.

The last class of investing is ownership investing. This category of investing can either make you big time or break you big time. In other words, it presents the highest level of risk possible; but if successful, major profits can be made. Stocks are the most popular investments of this type. With stock, you now move into the position to own a portion of a company, which allows you the opportunity to gain major revenue if you consistently monitor it; but if not, volatility or the unpredictable changes happening in the market will tear your investment to pieces.

The son has now graduated high school and is getting ready to shift out of state into college. The father understands that temptation and tribulation will be stronger than ever now on his son, and the degree of risk for him to invest in his son grows even higher than before. It is no longer time for the son to just sit and study the investment, but time for him to expand it. With the son now about to stare the biggest trials in his life face to face without the guidance of his father – as if staring down the barrel of a 45-millimeter gun with his life at the will of a simple movement of an index finger – it is now time for him to show what he is made of. He now has the opportunity not just to carry on his last name, but also to "own" and expound upon the legacy that comes with it. He has been thoroughly trained and can now carry out in strength what his father knows in wisdom.

We have to resurrect and acknowledge the great words of astounding abolitionist, Frederick Douglas, when he stated (in a summarized format), "Wanting power without struggle is like wanting crops without rain." Certain things in life will never prevail until you properly learn to produce, meaning you have to go through struggles and figure out ways to conquer them for yourself. You are not only going to go through these struggles for just yourself and people with your last name, but also for the ones that hear the great works of your last name and desire guidance. This manifestation of direction will not take place if you choose to remain blinded by the negative influences that surround you.

Why appease ignorance when you can simulate profound intelligence? Why take the time to linger around people who are no good for your future? (When, in all actuality, you know that they will not change until you show them that a mental metamorphosis can very well take place in those with the odds against their favor.)

I have never heard of or witnessed a tree eat its own fruit; your gift will always be there to equip someone with the strength to continue...

Certain things that provide pleasure at this temporary moment nine times out of ten will not benefit us in the future. On the other hand, we in fact tend to stray away from things that usually complicate our lives a bit more, such as studying, sacrificing, and cutting off hindering people. These are the factors that mold us into becoming the successful sculptures for which many people travel across the world just to admire and in turn take away new inspiration.

I have never heard of or witnessed a tree eat its own fruit; your gift will always be there to equip someone with the strength to continue on the journey of finding his or hers. In other words, when you walk into your destiny, you inspire others to find theirs. The glow you give off will be so vibrant that others cannot help but to notice it. Imagine being in a hotel room at night with family members. Everyone falls asleep, and that next morning the person who wakes up first opens the blinds and the sun efficiently illuminates the entire room. At this point, it is extremely hard for anyone to fall back asleep because the sun has awakened and notified everyone that the time to sleep is now over and that it is time to get the next day started. Your gift is the exact same way. When people see you doing the right thing and turning your life in a positive direction, it becomes an inevitable wake up call for them, which is part of the investment you make into others.

> **Someone has to make the sacrificial aspiration to leap so that others can make the conscious effort to fly.**

Unfortunately, investments do not start by themselves. Someone has to make the sacrificial aspiration to leap so that others can make the conscious effort to fly. Often, many young men in this country grow up without a father figure in their lives, either due

to tragic incidents or by the cowardice actions of a man denying the challenge of raising someone better than himself. To those of you in this category, this chapter alone should ignite a fire so deeply within you that no person or failure can put out.

You have the opportunity to invest into your children what your father withdrew from you. Not only just your children, but also anyone who admires the person you are as well as what you represent. You have the chance to train them and allow them to receive the proper grooming along the way to make sure no matter how many trials come their direction, they will make it through. No matter how many people say they do not have what it takes to conquer what others yield to, they will stand tall and prove them wrong. No matter how many selfish pessimists withdraw their investments, they will continue to deposit into theirs. They do this not just for themselves anymore, but also for the ones who now look up to them. Simply by overcoming the temporary obstacles of inflation that tried to block you, you can now become the pioneer of a permanent investment that could result in an everlasting legacy.

CHAPTER 13

To the Son of an Absent Father

Sometimes, when a person speaks about what he or she has not personally lived out, his thoughts to some are discredited. But please allow me to share with you my observation. I don't seek to belittle or speak down to anyone because I too am not exempt from mistakes, as I mentioned in earlier chapters. However, I would like to encourage those sons who are without biological fathers in their life.

Most would say that many of the challenges of our young black males today are directly related to the wrong models they have been drawn to. It is amazing how some negative people are the ones who, out of all the positive images around, get the spotlight. Much of what we seek out has to do with money, power, and sex. These are the catalytic or stimulating forces that drive so many young men's decisions. Yes, decisions are the measuring sticks that determine our rise or fall; our success or the lack

Yes, decisions are the measuring sticks that determine our rise or fall; our success or the lack thereof.

thereof. One of the crucial roles of a father to a son is to measure his son's degree of training and preparation when the son is about to make meaningful decisions in life.

There is a popular proverb that says train up a child in the way he should go, and when he is old he won't depart from it. Well, the truth is that there is little training without teachers, and that is part of my claim in the absence of fathers. So what is it that so many have to do in order to endure this missing component of life? You've got it – find another positive source!

Trust me: these sources, or resources, may be few; but they are out there. There are associations like the Boys and Girls Club and other church or community groups. There again, I am hoping that the My Brother's

Keeper initiative launched by President Barack Obama focuses on these needed resources.

However, some are destined to succeed, while most have to be determined to succeed. Each of us, no matter our background or family, has to encourage ourselves at times and say it's not over until I win. There are a lot of success stories where there was no dad at home but more so a brave courageous mom, grandparents, or a guardian who loved unconditionally. Yes, we are responsible for staying in the game. There are times you will get knocked down, but it is your responsibility to get up and learn from it. You also have to be determined to be to someone else what you've never had.

> **There are times you will get knocked down, but it is your responsibility to get up and learn from it.**

That's how you know you've made it – when you have helped to make others.

I have realized that growing up I have been nothing short of blessed to have my father in my life, but I could not finish this book until I gave my brothers that are lacking a father the strength to become one. I have many close friends that yearn for the presence of their fathers, but for numerous reasons have not been able to establish a relationship with them. The reasons go down the line from death to just having a dead-beat dad who is either locked up or just made the coward decision not to be in his son's life. With that being said, there is one thing that I want you to know. You will become what your father chose not to be; you crave to become what your father did not get the chance to be in your life; and you will be able to start a legacy for your last name that no man can tarnish. You must understand who you are, embrace the pain of where you are, and establish a new legacy that will tell who you were.

I have included the following scenario to paint a vivid picture of how I imagine it must be for a son to grow up without a father in the home: As a young child you are staying the night at your friend's house. It is approaching eight o'clock and you attentively watch as everyone gathers downstairs for dinner. Your friend's father arrives home after working overtime. He walks in, kisses his wife, hangs up his coat, sits down, and then tells everyone to grab hands and bow their heads to say grace. He begins by giving thanks for the protection of his family and yet another moment to spend with each other, then eventually goes on to give thanks for the food. As everyone begins to dig in, he asks everybody how their day has gone, and the conversation lasts until they finally finish eating. It is now time for you and your friend to get ready for bed.

Your friend's father walks in tells you good night, and then walks over to his son, rubs him on the head as he pulls up his covers and says, "Goodnight son; I love you." With your eyes closed at this point, you imagine that those last three words were meant for you. Squeezing your eyes tighter by the second, you try to make this moment last as long as possible because the moment you wake up, the fantasy ends and it is time to go home. It is time to go home where daddy never walks in from work. It is time to go home where daddy is never there to squeeze your hand in heartfelt sincerity and give thanks for your being in his life. It is time to come home where daddy never says goodnight, and leaves you sleepless in search of those three words that could put you to sleep like never before, "I love you."

In reality, you have encountered, are currently encountering, or will encounter a position of mental brokenness. At some point you have awakened and yearned for the presence of a deep voice in your home that could walk in and tell you and your siblings that you have nothing to worry about, "Daddy has you." You have yearned for someone to come home from work, throw all his baggage on the couch, run up to your mother, gently kiss her on the head and whisper to her that she is the queen that makes his entire world rotate on an axis of love that nobody could ever come in the way of. You've yearned for someone to show you what it means to be a true father, and you just so happen to call this man Dad.

Unfortunately, this is not the position you are in. You have been shorthanded unrightfully. You are in a position where you look amongst your peers with a perplexed gaze of guilt asking yourself, "Why did my father not want me?" Despite this state of antagonizing discomfort, you have to know who you are. You are a leader and nothing short of that. Who your father was does not make you who you are. Yes, you might have the same genes, but you certainly do not have to wear the same jeans or walk in the same shoes as he. Instinctively, this is a hard challenge to overcome because you are living the failure of your father.

> **Who your father was does not make you who you are.**

One of the greatest challenges of sons in ancient times, I can imagine, would be seeing their fathers lose in battle, transferring the burden to succeeding upon them whether they were ready or not. The difference between then and now is that ancient sons did not live in the pain; they embraced it to conquer everything that slew their fathers.

I can only fathom to an extent the pain of experiencing your father fail on bringing up someone who did not ask to be brought into this world. This pain has to be stored up daily to provide a burning fuel to go the extra mile in the classroom, in your sport, or in your household helping your mother. If anything, you want to take the pain away from her.

I cannot go any further in this section without commending the tremendous mothers throughout this nation who are raising families in a single parent household. Through all adversity they continue to be persistent on bending their backs every way to allow their children to climb on top of them and reach for the stars. Even though the male figure is not in the home, these magnificent women are committed to raising a male figure that will not only be examples to their children, but also to the world.

For this exact reason, you should take all the pain that you are encountering and put it in your gas tank for success. Take the pain of your mother away by handling your business so she will not have to worry about your being distracted. Take the pain of your siblings away by becoming an example that reminds them every time they seem to be distracted to get back on track. You take this pain and tear it up on the inside so your children will never have to. With every incident that attacks, you step on it, pick it up, and place it in the gas tank to give you the strength to go the extra mile that your father gave up on. It stands true that you may not have asked to come in this world, but by all means possible, you will let him know that you are here not by accident, but by destiny.

After you have taken every ounce of pain that tried to hold you back and turned it into fuel for finishing, it is time to become what you never had. It is time to step up to the plate, swing that bat, and knock your past out of the park to a point where you can still see it, but it can never return. As a matter of fact, the next time you are driving a car, take notice of this. In every car, the windshield happens to be bigger than the rearview mirror. The message behind this is that where you are going is way more important than where you have been. It is okay to occasionally look back and see the progress you have made, but you have

> **It is okay to occasionally look back and see the progress you have made, but you have to focus on what is ahead.**

to focus on what is ahead. At this point, you are ready to drive into a future that pain cannot hinder. You now can build a legacy from the ground up. You have the opportunity to become the man that travels places where people might not know him but have to respect him because they know his last name. They will also have to acknowledge the fact your first name is preceded by "Doctor."

Most importantly, you will be able to come home one day, throw all your bags on the couch, and have your wife run up to you jumping in your arms as you pick her up in affection and comfort. Then, placing her down, you will look her in the eyes and say, "The reason I work harder than anyone else in the world is because my queen deserves the world." Kissing her on the head, you will then walk away and head to your son's room. He will be peacefully sleeping after a long

> **For the love of a father outweighs the hate of the world at any cost.**

first day of kindergarten. Pulling up his covers and kissing him on the head, you will whisper, "Goodnight, Son. Daddy loves you." You will be at the point of no return. You will have conquered what your dad chose not to. Fear only attacks the hearts of those who already

147

have the ability to overcome, but you will have chosen to finish what he had no intention of starting. With that kiss and those three words, you will have established a father for years to come and a legacy for generations to follow. For the love of a father outweighs the hate of the world at any cost.

CHAPTER 14

Moving Forward

(The Conclusion)

As I attempt to wrap up this timeless thought, I trust with sincerity that all have been able to look through the thought in my literary discussion and unveil truth that, if embraced, would allow us to move forward. This was not an attempt to be rhetorical, but rather thought provoking and solution stimulating. In order to fulfill my purpose, I first elaborated on the significance of sonship; then examined the problem that hinders the emergence of America's future generations; and finally expounded on the remedy, which involves developing a mindset characterized by a positive change in thinking and behavior.

This book is not a black cause; it is a right cause. So often we want to color or frame something in a specific light, but doing so, in my opinion, only limits our view of the real issue. Why hold color over someone who breathes the same colorless oxygen as you? Oppression is not on one group of people; unfortunately, it finds its way to many ethnicities. I'm sure it's very safe to say that there is bigotry in almost every sector within the human race because prejudice stems from one's own low self worth. Prejudice is a product of the intimidation felt when encountering others who are different. I have come to understand that I do not have to hate or look down upon someone else to feel better about myself. When you are sure of your ability, you don't have to wish inability on others. In other words, become confident in what you know you are good at doing, and that confidence will enable you to strengthen others. To say this book is about just black sons would be easy; however, it is not. This book addresses all sons who should be given a chance to make the world a better place.

> **Prejudice is a product of the intimidation felt when encountering others who are different.**

One of the amazing history lessons I learned during my first week on the campus of Morehouse College was that a white man provided the financial funds to start my institution. In 1867, Rev. William Jefferson founded Augusta Theological Institute, which eventually became Morehouse College, named after Henry L. Morehouse, who provided the funds ("Morehouse Legacy"). The college began as a black institution to prepare former slaves for preaching and teaching. Most would not have fathomed that a historically black college would have been helped to start by a Caucasian, but this has been the case several times for black educational institutions known as HBCUs. This fact just goes to show that all people are not evil and self-centered; some people genuinely care about the well-being of others, even when they don't look like them. Such caring people realize that humanity is bigger than they are.

I do believe that many people have reached an understanding that America cannot flourish unless all Americans come together, not as one race, but as one nation of people with unlimited opportunity. Only a few narrow minded people ignorantly exercise sweeping generalizations and say that all people of a certain nationality, race, or cultural belief are convinced of the same ideals. I do believe that there are sensitive, caring and loving people of all walks of life. The mission is to find them and usher them to the surface of politics, media, education, economics, judicial systems, corporations and social services.

America should not be a melting pot, but more so a stew in which each ingredient keeps its own identity and purpose. In a melting pot, everything is the same, but within a stew is independence for a united cause. How can I say I love this country and not love the diverse aspects that make it America? It is impossible. It is America because of the freedom it constitutionally stands for. It is America because of the opportunities it promises to afford. It is America because it is the welcome center for those who want better and are willing to uphold its principles. It is America because we believe that all men were created equal. It is America because of the allowance of democracy. So, if you say you love America, you must love who she is and not just love what you wish her to become. As an American, you must embrace the conditions you agree with, and as far as the ones you disagree with, J.F.K. stated it best: "Ask

> **How can I say I love this country and not love the diverse aspects that make it America?**

not what your country can do for you, but what you can do for your country."

Although life is often filled with riddles that we must solve in order to move on to the next phase in our lives, we have to reverence the value of the names we carry along the journey. For a leader, the name means something greater than riches or glory of any kind. It represents and birth's legacy, something that is quite priceless and frankly irreplaceable. As we begin to accept the promise and baggage that comes with the name you know, we will begin to realize that we are next in line to be the change that everyone wants to see in our country.

Before we can effectively effect change, we must face the reality of the world that is so often evaded and rarely challenged. This reality includes matters such as the horrible judicial imbalance within this nation. By facing this reality presently, we can prevent youth from being victims of this fiasco in the future. This will encourage the disenfranchised sons and

Time is the one thing no man can alter to appease the course of his schedule.

daughters to make legacies for their last names in spite of the political unrest that tried to hinder them. The only factor that stands between them as well as everyone else in pursuit of their dreams is the element of time. Time is the one thing no man can alter to appease the course of his schedule. Therefore, we must accept the challenge that our time is now to make a difference. No one can do it for us. We have to do the dirty work ourselves. It is time to remove the metaphorical hoodie from over our heads, as well as the stereotypical hoodie from our hearts. Then, once this process is complete, we can finally begin preparing ourselves for the power that will be essential to make the change. After going through the proper preparations, you will be ready to transfer the benefits of your hard work on to someone else in the form of an investment. To those who had no one to invest in them, this is the time now to gear your focus into creating an investment to release into someone else's life – someone who had no one to pour into him or her. It is time to throw away the temporary hurt, to create legacy that will last forever. As for me, I accept the rigorous challenge of throwing away all the hatred that exists in my heart to create a love so strong for this nation that no stereotype, judicial imbalance, or political

> **In order to become a superlative nation, we must first become superlative natives with the best interest of the country at heart.**

unrest can come in the way of. By doing this, I believe that I will be bound to traveling the path of success that comes with being a part of this great nation.

We live in an enormous world filled with opportunities for greatness that all of us deserve no matter our nationality or gender. Therefore, we should come together as one nation to help the person next to us, not tear him or her down. In order to become a superlative nation, we must first become superlative natives with the best interest of the country at heart. We become great natives by accepting the modern diversity that comes with the privilege of opportunity in this country and releasing the anger that captivated our minds throughout the previous years of this land. It is time now to finally come together as one nation, under God, indivisible with liberty and justice for all.

ABOUT THE AUTHOR

Brandon B. Porter II is the son of Melody G. Porter and Bishop Brandon B. Porter, Sr., who pastors a prominent church in Memphis, Tennessee, and serves on the board of directors for the Church of God in Christ, Inc., an organization with over six million members expanding to over 63 countries. His grandfather, the late Bishop W.L. Porter, was also a renowned religious, community, and business leader.

Following in the vein of his father and his grandfather, Brandon II has already proven a desire to both lead and serve others. He currently attends Morehouse College in Atlanta, Georgia, where he exemplifies his innate leadership abilities. A second-year business major with a concentration in finance, Brandon was 1 of 12 selected from the entire Morehouse Business Association to be a protégé member. He was also a previous member of the Vanguard Leadership Program and currently serves on the elections committee for the Student Government Association at Morehouse College. A promising musician, Brandon received much inspiration from his great uncle, David Porter, a renowned songwriter and former vice-president of the famous Stax Records in Memphis, Tennessee

Brandon received recognition from Mark Luttrell, the mayor of Shelby County, for active services within the community through the STS (Setting the Standard) Organization. To sharpen his business savvy, he interned for Laurence V. Plummer Financial Services, a subsidiary of John Hancock Financial. He also served with the Memphis Youth and Career Development Program as well as the Future Business Leaders of America.

Entering into his sophomore year at Morehouse, Brandon received inspiration to write from his father, who has authored several books of his own. Brandon desires, through his writing, to motivate his generation to abandon helplessness and hopelessness and emerge as leaders who would make significant accomplishments in order to leave lasting legacies for generations to come. His seeks to remain an example for others, especially his younger brother Bryson, who Brandon deems as his greatest inspiration.

REFERENCES

"Abraham Lincoln." *Wikipedia: The Free Encyclopedia*. Wikimedia Foundation, Inc., 8 October 2014. Web. 11 Aug. 2014.

Alcindor, Yamiche. "Police Seek Order As Ferguson Furor Builds." *USA Today* 14 Aug. 2014: A1. Print

Boukus, Ellyn R., Alwyn Cassil, and Ann S. O'Malley. "A Snapshot of U.S. Physicians: Key Findings from the 2008 Health Tracking Physician Survey." *Hschange.com.* Septembe 2009. Web. 15 July 2014.

"Charles Richard Drew." *Bio.* A&E Television Networks, 2014. Web. 3 Sep. 2014.

Dahler, Don. "Bats' Future Hangs in the Balance as Deadly Disease Spreads." *CBSNews.com.* 5 Aug. 2014 Web. 30 Sep. 2014.

"Famous Black Inventors: A Rich Heritage Gives Way to Modern Ingenuity." *Black-Inventor.com.* Web. 3 Sep. 2014.

Fletcher, Michael A. "Networking tied to black jobless rate." Washington Post. 14 December 2012. Web. 02 July 2014.

"Garrett Augustus Morgan Sr." *Bio.* A&E Television Networks, 2014. Web. 3 Sep. 2014.

"George Washington Carver." *Bio.* A&E Television Networks, 2014. Web. 3 Sep. 2014.

Gray, Derwin. "#Ferguson, Why We Need More Multi-Ethnic Churches."n.p. 15 Aug. 2014. Web. 20 Aug. 2014.

Holland, Joshua. "A New Glass Ceiling? Why African-American Politicians Face an Uphill Battle for Senate Seats and Governorships." *Blackpoliticsontheweb.com* 21 March 2012. Web. 22 July 2014.

"Jackie Robinson West Little League Team Has Become the 'Pride of Chicago.'" *Huffingtonpost.com.23* Aug 2014. Web. 15 July 2014.

"Morehouse Legacy." *Morehouse.edu.* n.d. Web. 7 Aug 2014.

"Photographer Describes Capturing Iconic JFK Jr. Image." *Newyork.cbslocal.com.* 21 November 2013. Web. 22 July 2014.

Sherley. "THE ULTIMATE TROPHY: What the Phenomenon of Sports WAGS tells us about Sexism, Race and Beauty." *iamsherleyfierce.com.* 18Aug. 2014. Web. 15 July 2014.

"THE SIXTIES: The Long March to Freedom." *CNN.com – Transcripts*. 12 July 2014. Web. 30 Sep. 2014.